## Praise for *Effe* [illegible]

"Each item in Slatkin [illegible] ained lesson with its own source code. This makes the book random-access: Items are easy to browse and study in whatever order the reader needs. I will be recommending *Effective Python* to students as an admirably compact source of mainstream advice on a very broad range of topics for the intermediate Python programmer."

*—Brandon Rhodes, software engineer at Dropbox and chair of PyCon 2016-2017*

"I've been programming in Python for years and thought I knew it pretty well. Thanks to this treasure trove of tips and techniques, I realize there's so much more I could be doing with my Python code to make it faster (e.g., using built-in data structures), easier to read (e.g., enforcing keyword-only arguments), and much more Pythonic (e.g., using zip to iterate over lists in parallel)."

*—Pamela Fox, educationeer, Khan Academy*

"If I had this book when I first switched from Java to Python, it would have saved me many months of repeated code rewrites, which happened each time I realized I was doing particular things 'non-Pythonically.' This book collects the vast majority of basic Python 'must-knows' into one place, eliminating the need to stumble upon them one-by-one over the course of months or years. The scope of the book is impressive, starting with the importance of PEP8 as well as that of major Python idioms, then reaching through function, method and class design, effective standard library use, quality API design, testing, and performance measurement—this book really has it all. A fantastic introduction to what it really means to be a Python programmer for both the novice and the experienced developer."

*—Mike Bayer, creator of SQLAlchemy*

"*Effective Python* will take your Python skills to the next level with clear guidelines for improving Python code style and function."

*—Leah Culver, developer advocate, Dropbox*

"This book is an exceptionally great resource for seasoned developers in other languages who are looking to quickly pick up Python and move beyond the basic language constructs into more Pythonic code. The organization of the book is clear, concise, and easy to digest, and each item and chapter can stand on its own as a meditation on a particular topic. The book covers the breadth of language constructs in pure Python without confusing the reader with the complexities of the broader Python ecosystem. For more seasoned developers the book provides in-depth examples of language constructs they may not have previously encountered, and provides examples of less commonly used language features. It is clear that the author is exceptionally facile with Python, and he uses his professional experience to alert the reader to common subtle bugs and common failure modes. Furthermore, the book does an excellent job of pointing out subtleties between Python 2.X and Python 3.X and could serve as a refresher course as one transitions between variants of Python."

*—Katherine Scott, software lead, Tempo Automation*

"This is a great book for both novice and experienced programmers. The code examples and explanations are well thought out and explained concisely and thoroughly."

*—C. Titus Brown, associate professor, UC Davis*

"This is an immensely useful resource for advanced Python usage and building cleaner, more maintainable software. Anyone looking to take their Python skills to the next level would benefit from putting the book's advice into practice."

*—Wes McKinney, creator of pandas; author of* Python for Data Analysis; *and software engineer at Cloudera*

# Effective Python

# Effective Python

## 59 SPECIFIC WAYS TO WRITE BETTER PYTHON

Brett Slatkin

PEARSON

ISBN 978-93-325-5236-4

**First Impression, 2015**



Published by Pearson India Education Services Pvt.Ltd,CIN:U72200TN2005PTC057128.
Formerly known as TutorVista Global Pvt Ltd, licensees of Pearson Education in South Asia

Head Office:15th Floor, Tower-B, World Trade Tower, Plot No. 1, Block-C,Sector 16,
Noida 201 301, Uttar Pradesh, India

Registered Office: Module G4, Ground Floor, Elnet Software City, TS -140,Block 2 & 9
Rajiv Gandhi Salai, Taramani, Chennai, Tamil Nadu 600113.,Fax: 080-30461003,
Phone: 080-30461060, www.pearson.co.in email id: companysecretary.india@pearson.com

Digitally printed in India by CMS IT Services Private Limited, New Delhi in the year of 201

*To our family, loved and lost*

# Contents

# Preface

The Python programming language has unique strengths and charms that can be hard to grasp. Many programmers familiar with other languages often approach Python from a limited mindset instead of embracing its full expressivity. Some programmers go too far in the other direction, overusing Python features that can cause big problems later.

This book provides insight into the *Pythonic* way of writing programs: the best way to use Python. It builds on a fundamental understanding of the language that I assume you already have. Novice programmers will learn the best practices of Python's capabilities. Experienced programmers will learn how to embrace the strangeness of a new tool with confidence.

My goal is to prepare you to make a big impact with Python.

## What This Book Covers

Each chapter in this book contains a broad but related set of items. Feel free to jump between items and follow your interest. Each item contains concise and specific guidance explaining how you can write Python programs more effectively. Items include advice on what to do, what to avoid, how to strike the right balance, and why this is the best choice.

The items in this book are for Python 3 and Python 2 programmers alike (see Item 1: "Know Which Version of Python You're Using"). Programmers using alternative runtimes like Jython, IronPython, or PyPy should also find the majority of items to be applicable.

### Chapter 1: Pythonic Thinking

The Python community has come to use the adjective *Pythonic* to describe code that follows a particular style. The idioms of Python have emerged over time through experience using the language and working with others. This chapter covers the best way to do the most common things in Python.

**Chapter 2: Functions**

Functions in Python have a variety of extra features that make a programmer's life easier. Some are similar to capabilities in other programming languages, but many are unique to Python. This chapter covers how to use functions to clarify intention, promote reuse, and reduce bugs.

**Chapter 3: Classes and Inheritance**

Python is an object-oriented language. Getting things done in Python often requires writing new classes and defining how they interact through their interfaces and hierarchies. This chapter covers how to use classes and inheritance to express your intended behaviors with objects.

**Chapter 4: Metaclasses and Attributes**

Metaclasses and dynamic attributes are powerful Python features. However, they also enable you to implement extremely bizarre and unexpected behaviors. This chapter covers the common idioms for using these mechanisms to ensure that you follow the *rule of least surprise*.

**Chapter 5: Concurrency and Parallelism**

Python makes it easy to write concurrent programs that do many different things seemingly at the same time. Python can also be used to do parallel work through system calls, subprocesses, and C-extensions. This chapter covers how to best utilize Python in these subtly different situations.

**Chapter 6: Built-in Modules**

Python is installed with many of the important modules that you'll need to write programs. These standard packages are so closely intertwined with idiomatic Python that they may as well be part of the language specification. This chapter covers the essential built-in modules.

**Chapter 7: Collaboration**

Collaborating on Python programs requires you to be deliberate about how you write your code. Even if you're working alone, you'll want to understand how to use modules written by others. This chapter covers the standard tools and best practices that enable people to work together on Python programs.

**Chapter 8: Production**

Python has facilities for adapting to multiple deployment environments. It also has built-in modules that aid in hardening your programs and making them bulletproof. This chapter covers how to use Python to debug, optimize, and test your programs to maximize quality and performance at runtime.

## Conventions Used in This Book

Python code snippets in this book are in `monospace font` and have syntax highlighting. I take some artistic license with the Python style guide to make the code examples better fit the format of a book or to highlight the most important parts. When lines are long, I use ➥ characters to indicate that they wrap. I truncate snippets with ellipses comments (#. . .) to indicate regions where code exists that isn't essential for expressing the point. I've also left out embedded documentation to reduce the size of code examples. I strongly suggest that you don't do this in your projects; instead, you should follow the style guide (see Item 2: "Follow the PEP 8 Style Guide") and write documentation (see Item 49: "Write Docstrings for Every Function, Class, and Module").

Most code snippets in this book are accompanied by the corresponding output from running the code. When I say "output," I mean console or terminal output: what you see when running the Python program in an interactive interpreter. Output sections are in monospace font and are preceded by a >>> line (the Python interactive prompt). The idea is that you could type the code snippets into a Python shell and reproduce the expected output.

Finally, there are some other sections in monospace font that are not preceded by a >>> line. These represent the output of running programs besides the Python interpreter. These examples often begin with $ characters to indicate that I'm running programs from a command-line shell like Bash.

## Where to Get the Code and Errata

It's useful to view some of the examples in this book as whole programs without interleaved prose. This also gives you a chance to tinker with the code yourself and understand why the program works as described. You can find the source code for all code snippets in this book on the book's website (http://www.effectivepython.com). Any errors found in the book will have corrections posted on the website.

# Acknowledgments

This book would not have been possible without the guidance, support, and encouragement from many people in my life.

Thanks to Scott Meyers for the Effective Software Development series. I first read *Effective C++* when I was 15 years old and fell in love with the language. There's no doubt that Scott's books led to my academic experience and first job at Google. I'm thrilled to have had the opportunity to write this book.

Thanks to my core technical reviewers for the depth and thoroughness of their feedback: Brett Cannon, Tavis Rudd, and Mike Taylor. Thanks to Leah Culver and Adrian Holovaty for thinking this book would be a good idea. Thanks to my friends who patiently read earlier versions of this book: Michael Levine, Marzia Niccolai, Ade Oshineye, and Katrina Sostek. Thanks to my colleagues at Google for their review. Without all of your help, this book would have been inscrutable.

Thanks to everyone involved in making this book a reality. Thanks to my editor Trina MacDonald for kicking off the process and being supportive throughout. Thanks to the team who were instrumental: development editors Tom Cirtin and Chris Zahn, editorial assistant Olivia Basegio, marketing manager Stephane Nakib, copy editor Stephanie Geels, and production editor Julie Nahil.

Thanks to the wonderful Python programmers I've known and worked with: Anthony Baxter, Brett Cannon, Wesley Chun, Jeremy Hylton, Alex Martelli, Neal Norwitz, Guido van Rossum, Andy Smith, Greg Stein, and Ka-Ping Yee. I appreciate your tutelage and leadership. Python has an excellent community and I feel lucky to be a part of it.

Thanks to my teammates over the years for letting me be the worst player in the band. Thanks to Kevin Gibbs for helping me take risks. Thanks to Ken Ashcraft, Ryan Barrett, and Jon McAlister for showing me how it's done. Thanks to Brad Fitzpatrick for taking it to the next level. Thanks to Paul McDonald for co-founding our crazy project. Thanks to Jeremy Ginsberg and Jack Hebert for making it a reality.

Thanks to the inspiring programming teachers I've had: Ben Chelf, Vince Hugo, Russ Lewin, Jon Stemmle, Derek Thomson, and Daniel Wang. Without your instruction, I would never have pursued our craft or gained the perspective required to teach others.

Thanks to my mother for giving me a sense of purpose and encouraging me to become a programmer. Thanks to my brother, my grandparents, and the rest of my family and childhood friends for being role models as I grew up and found my passion.

Finally, thanks to my wife, Colleen, for her love, support, and laughter through the journey of life.

# About the Author

**Brett Slatkin** is a senior staff software engineer at Google. He is the engineering lead and co-founder of Google Consumer Surveys. He formerly worked on Google App Engine's Python infrastructure. He is the co-creator of the PubSubHubbub protocol. Nine years ago he cut his teeth using Python to manage Google's enormous fleet of servers.

Outside of his day job, he works on open source tools and writes about software, bicycles, and other topics on his personal website (http://onebigfluke.com). He earned his B.S. in computer engineering from Columbia University in the City of New York. He lives in San Francisco.

# 1 Pythonic Thinking

The idioms of a programming language are defined by its users. Over the years, the Python community has come to use the adjective *Pythonic* to describe code that follows a particular style. The Pythonic style isn't regimented or enforced by the compiler. It has emerged over time through experience using the language and working with others. Python programmers prefer to be explicit, to choose simple over complex, and to maximize readability (type `import this`).

Programmers familiar with other languages may try to write Python as if it's C++, Java, or whatever they know best. New programmers may still be getting comfortable with the vast range of concepts expressible in Python. It's important for everyone to know the best—the *Pythonic*—way to do the most common things in Python. These patterns will affect every program you write.

## Item 1: Know Which Version of Python You're Using

Throughout this book, the majority of example code is in the syntax of Python 3.4 (released March 17, 2014). This book also provides some examples in the syntax of Python 2.7 (released July 3, 2010) to highlight important differences. Most of my advice applies to all of the popular Python runtimes: CPython, Jython, IronPython, PyPy, etc.

Many computers come with multiple versions of the standard CPython runtime preinstalled. However, the default meaning of `python` on the command-line may not be clear. `python` is usually an alias for `python2.7`, but it can sometimes be an alias for older versions like `python2.6` or `python2.5`. To find out exactly which version of Python you're using, you can use the `--version` flag.

```
$ python --version
Python 2.7.8
```

Python 3 is usually available under the name python3.

```
$ python3 --version
Python 3.4.2
```

You can also figure out the version of Python you're using at runtime by inspecting values in the sys built-in module.

```
import sys
print(sys.version_info)
print(sys.version)

>>>
sys.version_info(major=3, minor=4, micro=2,
➥releaselevel='final', serial=0)
3.4.2 (default, Oct 19 2014, 17:52:17)
[GCC 4.2.1 Compatible Apple LLVM 6.0 (clang-600.0.51)]
```

Python 2 and Python 3 are both actively maintained by the Python community. Development on Python 2 is frozen beyond bug fixes, security improvements, and backports to ease the transition from Python 2 to Python 3. Helpful tools like the 2to3 and six exist to make it easier to adopt Python 3 going forward.

Python 3 is constantly getting new features and improvements that will never be added to Python 2. As of the writing of this book, the majority of Python's most common open source libraries are compatible with Python 3. I strongly encourage you to use Python 3 for your next Python project.

### Things to Remember

- ✦ There are two major versions of Python still in active use: Python 2 and Python 3.
- ✦ There are multiple popular runtimes for Python: CPython, Jython, IronPython, PyPy, etc.
- ✦ Be sure that the command-line for running Python on your system is the version you expect it to be.
- ✦ Prefer Python 3 for your next project because that is the primary focus of the Python community.

## Item 2: Follow the PEP 8 Style Guide

Python Enhancement Proposal #8, otherwise known as PEP 8, is the style guide for how to format Python code. You are welcome to write Python code however you want, as long as it has valid syntax.

However, using a consistent style makes your code more approachable and easier to read. Sharing a common style with other Python programmers in the larger community facilitates collaboration on projects. But even if you are the only one who will ever read your code, following the style guide will make it easier to change things later.

PEP 8 has a wealth of details about how to write clear Python code. It continues to be updated as the Python language evolves. It's worth reading the whole guide online (http://www.python.org/dev/peps/pep-0008/). Here are a few rules you should be sure to follow:

**Whitespace:** In Python, whitespace is syntactically significant. Python programmers are especially sensitive to the effects of whitespace on code clarity.

- Use spaces instead of tabs for indentation.
- Use four spaces for each level of syntactically significant indenting.
- Lines should be 79 characters in length or less.
- Continuations of long expressions onto additional lines should be indented by four extra spaces from their normal indentation level.
- In a file, functions and classes should be separated by two blank lines.
- In a class, methods should be separated by one blank line.
- Don't put spaces around list indexes, function calls, or keyword argument assignments.
- Put one—and only one—space before and after variable assignments.

**Naming:** PEP 8 suggests unique styles of naming for different parts in the language. This makes it easy to distinguish which type corresponds to each name when reading code.

- Functions, variables, and attributes should be in `lowercase_underscore` format.
- Protected instance attributes should be in `_leading_underscore` format.
- Private instance attributes should be in `__double_leading_underscore` format.
- Classes and exceptions should be in `CapitalizedWord` format.
- Module-level constants should be in `ALL_CAPS` format.

- Instance methods in classes should use `self` as the name of the first parameter (which refers to the object).
- Class methods should use `cls` as the name of the first parameter (which refers to the class).

**Expressions and Statements:** *The Zen of Python* states: "There should be one—and preferably only one—obvious way to do it." PEP 8 attempts to codify this style in its guidance for expressions and statements.

- Use inline negation (`if a is not b`) instead of negation of positive expressions (`if not a is b`).
- Don't check for empty values (like `[]` or `''`) by checking the length (`if len(somelist) == 0`). Use `if not somelist` and assume empty values implicitly evaluate to `False`.
- The same thing goes for non-empty values (like `[1]` or `'hi'`). The statement `if somelist` is implicitly `True` for non-empty values.
- Avoid single-line `if` statements, `for` and `while` loops, and `except` compound statements. Spread these over multiple lines for clarity.
- Always put `import` statements at the top of a file.
- Always use absolute names for modules when importing them, not names relative to the current module's own path. For example, to import the `foo` module from the `bar` package, you should do `from bar import foo`, not just `import foo`.
- If you must do relative imports, use the explicit syntax `from . import foo`.
- Imports should be in sections in the following order: standard library modules, third-party modules, your own modules. Each subsection should have imports in alphabetical order.

Note

The Pylint tool (http://www.pylint.org/) is a popular static analyzer for Python source code. Pylint provides automated enforcement of the PEP 8 style guide and detects many other types of common errors in Python programs.

### Things to Remember

- ✦ Always follow the PEP 8 style guide when writing Python code.
- ✦ Sharing a common style with the larger Python community facilitates collaboration with others.
- ✦ Using a consistent style makes it easier to modify your own code later.

## Item 3: Know the Differences Between bytes, str, and unicode

In Python 3, there are two types that represent sequences of characters: bytes and str. Instances of bytes contain raw 8-bit values. Instances of str contain Unicode characters.

In Python 2, there are two types that represent sequences of characters: str and unicode. In contrast to Python 3, instances of str contain raw 8-bit values. Instances of unicode contain Unicode characters.

There are many ways to represent Unicode characters as binary data (raw 8-bit values). The most common encoding is *UTF-8*. Importantly, str instances in Python 3 and unicode instances in Python 2 do not have an associated binary encoding. To convert Unicode characters to binary data, you must use the encode method. To convert binary data to Unicode characters, you must use the decode method.

When you're writing Python programs, it's important to do encoding and decoding of Unicode at the furthest boundary of your interfaces. The core of your program should use Unicode character types (str in Python 3, unicode in Python 2) and should not assume anything about character encodings. This approach allows you to be very accepting of alternative text encodings (such as *Latin-1*, *Shift JIS*, and *Big5*) while being strict about your output text encoding (ideally, UTF-8).

The split between character types leads to two common situations in Python code:

- You want to operate on raw 8-bit values that are UTF-8-encoded characters (or some other encoding).
- You want to operate on Unicode characters that have no specific encoding.

You'll often need two helper functions to convert between these two cases and to ensure that the type of input values matches your code's expectations.

In Python 3, you'll need one method that takes a str or bytes and always returns a str.

```
def to_str(bytes_or_str):
    if isinstance(bytes_or_str, bytes):
        value = bytes_or_str.decode('utf-8')
    else:
        value = bytes_or_str
    return value  # Instance of str
```

You'll need another method that takes a str or bytes and always returns a bytes.

```
def to_bytes(bytes_or_str):
    if isinstance(bytes_or_str, str):
        value = bytes_or_str.encode('utf-8')
    else:
        value = bytes_or_str
    return value  # Instance of bytes
```

In Python 2, you'll need one method that takes a str or unicode and always returns a unicode.

```
# Python 2
def to_unicode(unicode_or_str):
    if isinstance(unicode_or_str, str):
        value = unicode_or_str.decode('utf-8')
    else:
        value = unicode_or_str
    return value  # Instance of unicode
```

You'll need another method that takes str or unicode and always returns a str.

```
# Python 2
def to_str(unicode_or_str):
    if isinstance(unicode_or_str, unicode):
        value = unicode_or_str.encode('utf-8')
    else:
        value = unicode_or_str
    return value  # Instance of str
```

There are two big gotchas when dealing with raw 8-bit values and Unicode characters in Python.

The first issue is that in Python 2, unicode and str instances seem to be the same type when a str only contains 7-bit ASCII characters.

- You can combine such a str and unicode together using the + operator.
- You can compare such str and unicode instances using equality and inequality operators.
- You can use unicode instances for format strings like '%s'.

All of this behavior means that you can often pass a str or unicode instance to a function expecting one or the other and things will just work (as long as you're only dealing with 7-bit ASCII). In Python 3, bytes and str instances are never equivalent—not even the empty string—so you must be more deliberate about the types of character sequences that you're passing around.

The second issue is that in Python 3, operations involving file handles (returned by the open built-in function) default to UTF-8 encoding. In Python 2, file operations default to binary encoding. This causes surprising failures, especially for programmers accustomed to Python 2.

For example, say you want to write some random binary data to a file. In Python 2, this works. In Python 3, this breaks.

```
with open('/tmp/random.bin', 'w') as f:
    f.write(os.urandom(10))

>>>
TypeError: must be str, not bytes
```

The cause of this exception is the new `encoding` argument for `open` that was added in Python 3. This parameter defaults to `'utf-8'`. That makes `read` and `write` operations on file handles expect `str` instances containing Unicode characters instead of `bytes` instances containing binary data.

To make this work properly, you must indicate that the data is being opened in write binary mode (`'wb'`) instead of write character mode (`'w'`). Here, I use `open` in a way that works correctly in Python 2 and Python 3:

```
with open('/tmp/random.bin', 'wb') as f:
    f.write(os.urandom(10))
```

This problem also exists for reading data from files. The solution is the same: Indicate binary mode by using `'rb'` instead of `'r'` when opening a file.

### Things to Remember

✦ In Python 3, `bytes` contains sequences of 8-bit values, `str` contains sequences of Unicode characters. `bytes` and `str` instances can't be used together with operators (like > or +).

✦ In Python 2, `str` contains sequences of 8-bit values, `unicode` contains sequences of Unicode characters. `str` and `unicode` *can* be used together with operators if the `str` only contains 7-bit ASCII characters.

✦ Use helper functions to ensure that the inputs you operate on are the type of character sequence you expect (8-bit values, UTF-8 encoded characters, Unicode characters, etc.).

✦ If you want to read or write binary data to/from a file, always open the file using a binary mode (like `'rb'` or `'wb'`).

## Item 4: Write Helper Functions Instead of Complex Expressions

Python's pithy syntax makes it easy to write single-line expressions that implement a lot of logic. For example, say you want to decode the query string from a URL. Here, each query string parameter represents an integer value:

```
from urllib.parse import parse_qs
my_values = parse_qs('red=5&blue=0&green=',
                     keep_blank_values=True)
print(repr(my_values))

>>>
{'red': ['5'], 'green': [''], 'blue': ['0']}
```

Some query string parameters may have multiple values, some may have single values, some may be present but have blank values, and some may be missing entirely. Using the `get` method on the result dictionary will return different values in each circumstance.

```
print('Red:     ', my_values.get('red'))
print('Green:   ', my_values.get('green'))
print('Opacity: ', my_values.get('opacity'))

>>>
Red:     ['5']
Green:   ['']
Opacity: None
```

It'd be nice if a default value of `0` was assigned when a parameter isn't supplied or is blank. You might choose to do this with Boolean expressions because it feels like this logic doesn't merit a whole `if` statement or helper function quite yet.

Python's syntax makes this choice all too easy. The trick here is that the empty string, the empty list, and zero all evaluate to `False` implicitly. Thus, the expressions below will evaluate to the subexpression after the `or` operator when the first subexpression is `False`.

```
# For query string 'red=5&blue=0&green='
red = my_values.get('red', [''])[0] or 0
green = my_values.get('green', [''])[0] or 0
opacity = my_values.get('opacity', [''])[0] or 0
print('Red:     %r' % red)
print('Green:   %r' % green)
print('Opacity: %r' % opacity)
```

```
>>>
Red:     '5'
Green:   0
Opacity: 0
```

The red case works because the key is present in the my_values dictionary. The value is a list with one member: the string '5'. This string implicitly evaluates to True, so red is assigned to the first part of the or expression.

The green case works because the value in the my_values dictionary is a list with one member: an empty string. The empty string implicitly evaluates to False, causing the or expression to evaluate to 0.

The opacity case works because the value in the my_values dictionary is missing altogether. The behavior of the get method is to return its second argument if the key doesn't exist in the dictionary. The default value in this case is a list with one member, an empty string. When opacity isn't found in the dictionary, this code does exactly the same thing as the green case.

However, this expression is difficult to read and it still doesn't do everything you need. You'd also want to ensure that all the parameter values are integers so you can use them in mathematical expressions. To do that, you'd wrap each expression with the int built-in function to parse the string as an integer.

```
red = int(my_values.get('red', [''])[0] or 0)
```

This is now extremely hard to read. There's so much visual noise. The code isn't approachable. A new reader of the code would have to spend too much time picking apart the expression to figure out what it actually does. Even though it's nice to keep things short, it's not worth trying to fit this all on one line.

Python 2.5 added if/else conditional—or ternary—expressions to make cases like this clearer while keeping the code short.

```
red = my_values.get('red', [''])
red = int(red[0]) if red[0] else 0
```

This is better. For less complicated situations, if/else conditional expressions can make things very clear. But the example above is still not as clear as the alternative of a full if/else statement over multiple lines. Seeing all of the logic spread out like this makes the dense version seem even more complex.

```
green = my_values.get('green', [''])
if green[0]:
    green = int(green[0])
else:
    green = 0
```

Writing a helper function is the way to go, especially if you need to use this logic repeatedly.

```
def get_first_int(values, key, default=0):
    found = values.get(key, [''])
    if found[0]:
        found = int(found[0])
    else:
        found = default
    return found
```

The calling code is much clearer than the complex expression using `or` and the two-line version using the `if/else` expression.

```
green = get_first_int(my_values, 'green')
```

As soon as your expressions get complicated, it's time to consider splitting them into smaller pieces and moving logic into helper functions. What you gain in readability always outweighs what brevity may have afforded you. Don't let Python's pithy syntax for complex expressions get you into a mess like this.

### Things to Remember

- ✦ Python's syntax makes it all too easy to write single-line expressions that are overly complicated and difficult to read.
- ✦ Move complex expressions into helper functions, especially if you need to use the same logic repeatedly.
- ✦ The `if/else` expression provides a more readable alternative to using Boolean operators like `or` and `and` in expressions.

## Item 5: Know How to Slice Sequences

Python includes syntax for slicing sequences into pieces. Slicing lets you access a subset of a sequence's items with minimal effort. The simplest uses for slicing are the built-in types `list`, `str`, and `bytes`. Slicing can be extended to any Python class that implements the `__getitem__` and `__setitem__` special methods (see Item 28: "Inherit from `collections.abc` for Custom Container Types").

The basic form of the slicing syntax is somelist[start:end], where start is inclusive and end is exclusive.

```
a = ['a', 'b', 'c', 'd', 'e', 'f', 'g', 'h']
print('First four:', a[:4])
print('Last four: ', a[-4:])
print('Middle two:', a[3:-3])

>>>
First four: ['a', 'b', 'c', 'd']
Last four:  ['e', 'f', 'g', 'h']
Middle two: ['d', 'e']
```

When slicing from the start of a list, you should leave out the zero index to reduce visual noise.

```
assert a[:5] == a[0:5]
```

When slicing to the end of a list, you should leave out the final index because it's redundant.

```
assert a[5:] == a[5:len(a)]
```

Using negative numbers for slicing is helpful for doing offsets relative to the end of a list. All of these forms of slicing would be clear to a new reader of your code. There are no surprises, and I encourage you to use these variations.

```
a[:]      # ['a', 'b', 'c', 'd', 'e', 'f', 'g', 'h']
a[:5]     # ['a', 'b', 'c', 'd', 'e']
a[:-1]    # ['a', 'b', 'c', 'd', 'e', 'f', 'g']
a[4:]     #                     ['e', 'f', 'g', 'h']
a[-3:]    #                          ['f', 'g', 'h']
a[2:5]    #           ['c', 'd', 'e']
a[2:-1]   #           ['c', 'd', 'e', 'f', 'g']
a[-3:-1]  #                          ['f', 'g']
```

Slicing deals properly with start and end indexes that are beyond the boundaries of the list. That makes it easy for your code to establish a maximum length to consider for an input sequence.

```
first_twenty_items = a[:20]
last_twenty_items = a[-20:]
```

In contrast, accessing the same index directly causes an exception.

```
a[20]

>>>
IndexError: list index out of range
```

**Note**

Beware that indexing a list by a negative variable is one of the few situations in which you can get surprising results from slicing. For example, the expression `somelist[-n:]` will work fine when n is greater than one (e.g., `somelist[-3:]`). However, when n is zero, the expression `somelist[-0:]` will result in a copy of the original list.

The result of slicing a list is a whole new list. References to the objects from the original list are maintained. Modifying the result of slicing won't affect the original list.

```
b = a[4:]
print('Before:   ', b)
b[1] = 99
print('After:    ', b)
print('No change:', a)

>>>
Before:    ['e', 'f', 'g', 'h']
After:     ['e', 99, 'g', 'h']
No change: ['a', 'b', 'c', 'd', 'e', 'f', 'g', 'h']
```

When used in assignments, slices will replace the specified range in the original list. Unlike tuple assignments (like `a, b = c[:2]`), the length of slice assignments don't need to be the same. The values before and after the assigned slice will be preserved. The list will grow or shrink to accommodate the new values.

```
print('Before ', a)
a[2:7] = [99, 22, 14]
print('After  ', a)
>>>
Before  ['a', 'b', 'c', 'd', 'e', 'f', 'g', 'h']
After   ['a', 'b', 99, 22, 14, 'h']
```

If you leave out both the start and the end indexes when slicing, you'll end up with a copy of the original list.

```
b = a[:]
assert b == a and b is not a
```

If you assign a slice with no start or end indexes, you'll replace its entire contents with a copy of what's referenced (instead of allocating a new list).

```
b = a
print('Before', a)
a[:] = [101, 102, 103]
```

```
assert a is b              # Still the same list object
print('After ', a)         # Now has different contents

>>>
Before ['a', 'b', 99, 22, 14, 'h']
After  [101, 102, 103]
```

**Things to Remember**

- ✦ Avoid being verbose: Don't supply 0 for the start index or the length of the sequence for the end index.
- ✦ Slicing is forgiving of start or end indexes that are out of bounds, making it easy to express slices on the front or back boundaries of a sequence (like a[:20] or a[-20:]).
- ✦ Assigning to a list slice will replace that range in the original sequence with what's referenced even if their lengths are different.

## Item 6: Avoid Using start, end, and stride in a Single Slice

In addition to basic slicing (see Item 5: "Know How to Slice Sequences"), Python has special syntax for the stride of a slice in the form somelist[start:end:stride]. This lets you take every *n*th item when slicing a sequence. For example, the stride makes it easy to group by even and odd indexes in a list.

```
a = ['red', 'orange', 'yellow', 'green', 'blue', 'purple']
odds = a[::2]
evens = a[1::2]
print(odds)
print(evens)

>>>
['red', 'yellow', 'blue']
['orange', 'green', 'purple']
```

The problem is that the stride syntax often causes unexpected behavior that can introduce bugs. For example, a common Python trick for reversing a byte string is to slice the string with a stride of -1.

```
x = b'mongoose'
y = x[::-1]
print(y)

>>>
b'esoognom'
```

That works well for byte strings and ASCII characters, but it will break for Unicode characters encoded as UTF-8 byte strings.

```
w = '謝謝'
x = w.encode('utf-8')
y = x[::-1]
z = y.decode('utf-8')

>>>
UnicodeDecodeError: 'utf-8' codec can't decode byte 0x9d in
position 0: invalid start byte
```

Are negative strides besides -1 useful? Consider the following examples.

```
a = ['a', 'b', 'c', 'd', 'e', 'f', 'g', 'h']
a[::2]   # ['a', 'c', 'e', 'g']
a[::-2]  # ['h', 'f', 'd', 'b']
```

Here, ::2 means select every second item starting at the beginning. Trickier, ::-2 means select every second item starting at the end and moving backwards.

What do you think 2::2 means? What about -2::-2 vs. -2:2:-2 vs. 2:2:-2?

```
a[2::2]     # ['c', 'e', 'g']
a[-2::-2]   # ['g', 'e', 'c', 'a']
a[-2:2:-2]  # ['g', 'e']
a[2:2:-2]   # []
```

The point is that the `stride` part of the slicing syntax can be extremely confusing. Having three numbers within the brackets is hard enough to read because of its density. Then it's not obvious when the `start` and `end` indexes come into effect relative to the `stride` value, especially when `stride` is negative.

To prevent problems, avoid using `stride` along with `start` and `end` indexes. If you must use a `stride`, prefer making it a positive value and omit `start` and `end` indexes. If you must use `stride` with `start` or `end` indexes, consider using one assignment to stride and another to slice.

```
b = a[::2]   # ['a', 'c', 'e', 'g']
c = b[1:-1]  # ['c', 'e']
```

Slicing and then striding will create an extra shallow copy of the data. The first operation should try to reduce the size of the resulting slice by as much as possible. If your program can't afford the time or memory required for two steps, consider using the `itertools` built-in module's `islice` method (see Item 46: "Use Built-in Algorithms and Data Structures"), which doesn't permit negative values for `start`, `end`, or `stride`.

**Things to Remember**

- ✦ Specifying start, end, and stride in a slice can be extremely confusing.
- ✦ Prefer using positive stride values in slices without start or end indexes. Avoid negative stride values if possible.
- ✦ Avoid using start, end, and stride together in a single slice. If you need all three parameters, consider doing two assignments (one to slice, another to stride) or using islice from the itertools built-in module.

## Item 7: Use List Comprehensions Instead of map and filter

Python provides compact syntax for deriving one list from another. These expressions are called *list comprehensions*. For example, say you want to compute the square of each number in a list. You can do this by providing the expression for your computation and the input sequence to loop over.

```
a = [1, 2, 3, 4, 5, 6, 7, 8, 9, 10]
squares = [x**2 for x in a]
print(squares)

>>>
[1, 4, 9, 16, 25, 36, 49, 64, 81, 100]
```

Unless you're applying a single-argument function, list comprehensions are clearer than the map built-in function for simple cases. map requires creating a lambda function for the computation, which is visually noisy.

```
squares = map(lambda x: x ** 2, a)
```

Unlike map, list comprehensions let you easily filter items from the input list, removing corresponding outputs from the result. For example, say you only want to compute the squares of the numbers that are divisible by 2. Here, I do this by adding a conditional expression to the list comprehension after the loop:

```
even_squares = [x**2 for x in a if x % 2 == 0]
print(even_squares)

>>>
[4, 16, 36, 64, 100]
```

The filter built-in function can be used along with map to achieve the same outcome, but it is much harder to read.

```
alt = map(lambda x: x**2, filter(lambda x: x % 2 == 0, a))
assert even_squares == list(alt)
```

Dictionaries and sets have their own equivalents of list comprehensions. These make it easy to create derivative data structures when writing algorithms.

```
chile_ranks = {'ghost': 1, 'habanero': 2, 'cayenne': 3}
rank_dict = {rank: name for name, rank in chile_ranks.items()}
chile_len_set = {len(name) for name in rank_dict.values()}
print(rank_dict)
print(chile_len_set)

>>>
{1: 'ghost', 2: 'habanero', 3: 'cayenne'}
{8, 5, 7}
```

### Things to Remember

- ✦ List comprehensions are clearer than the `map` and `filter` built-in functions because they don't require extra `lambda` expressions.
- ✦ List comprehensions allow you to easily skip items from the input list, a behavior `map` doesn't support without help from `filter`.
- ✦ Dictionaries and sets also support comprehension expressions.

## Item 8: Avoid More Than Two Expressions in List Comprehensions

Beyond basic usage (see Item 7: "Use List Comprehensions Instead of `map` and `filter`"), list comprehensions also support multiple levels of looping. For example, say you want to simplify a matrix (a list containing other lists) into one flat list of all cells. Here, I do this with a list comprehension by including two `for` expressions. These expressions run in the order provided from left to right.

```
matrix = [[1, 2, 3], [4, 5, 6], [7, 8, 9]]
flat = [x for row in matrix for x in row]
print(flat)

>>>
[1, 2, 3, 4, 5, 6, 7, 8, 9]
```

The example above is simple, readable, and a reasonable usage of multiple loops. Another reasonable usage of multiple loops is replicating the two-level deep layout of the input list. For example, say you want to square the value in each cell of a two-dimensional matrix. This expression is noisier because of the extra `[]` characters, but it's still easy to read.

```
squared = [[x**2 for x in row] for row in matrix]
print(squared)

>>>
[[1, 4, 9], [16, 25, 36], [49, 64, 81]]
```

If this expression included another loop, the list comprehension would get so long that you'd have to split it over multiple lines.

```
my_lists = [
    [[1, 2, 3], [4, 5, 6]],
    # ...
]
flat = [x for sublist1 in my_lists
        for sublist2 in sublist1
        for x in sublist2]
```

At this point, the multiline comprehension isn't much shorter than the alternative. Here, I produce the same result using normal loop statements. The indentation of this version makes the looping clearer than the list comprehension.

```
flat = []
for sublist1 in my_lists:
    for sublist2 in sublist1:
        flat.extend(sublist2)
```

List comprehensions also support multiple `if` conditions. Multiple conditions at the same loop level are an implicit `and` expression. For example, say you want to filter a list of numbers to only even values greater than four. These two list comprehensions are equivalent.

```
a = [1, 2, 3, 4, 5, 6, 7, 8, 9, 10]
b = [x for x in a if x > 4 if x % 2 == 0]
c = [x for x in a if x > 4 and x % 2 == 0]
```

Conditions can be specified at each level of looping after the `for` expression. For example, say you want to filter a matrix so the only cells remaining are those divisible by 3 in rows that sum to 10 or higher. Expressing this with list comprehensions is short, but extremely difficult to read.

```
matrix = [[1, 2, 3], [4, 5, 6], [7, 8, 9]]
filtered = [[x for x in row if x % 3 == 0]
            for row in matrix if sum(row) >= 10]
print(filtered)

>>>
[[6], [9]]
```

Though this example is a bit convoluted, in practice you'll see situations arise where such expressions seem like a good fit. I strongly encourage you to avoid using list comprehensions that look like this. The resulting code is very difficult for others to comprehend. What you save in the number of lines doesn't outweigh the difficulties it could cause later.

The rule of thumb is to avoid using more than two expressions in a list comprehension. This could be two conditions, two loops, or one condition and one loop. As soon as it gets more complicated than that, you should use normal `if` and `for` statements and write a helper function (see Item 16: "Consider Generators Instead of Returning Lists").

### Things to Remember

- ✦ List comprehensions support multiple levels of loops and multiple conditions per loop level.
- ✦ List comprehensions with more than two expressions are very difficult to read and should be avoided.

## Item 9: Consider Generator Expressions for Large Comprehensions

The problem with list comprehensions (see Item 7: "Use List Comprehensions Instead of `map` and `filter`") is that they may create a whole new list containing one item for each value in the input sequence. This is fine for small inputs, but for large inputs this could consume significant amounts of memory and cause your program to crash.

For example, say you want to read a file and return the number of characters on each line. Doing this with a list comprehension would require holding the length of every line of the file in memory. If the file is absolutely enormous or perhaps a never-ending network socket, list comprehensions are problematic. Here, I use a list comprehension in a way that can only handle small input values.

```
value = [len(x) for x in open('/tmp/my_file.txt')]
print(value)

>>>
[100, 57, 15, 1, 12, 75, 5, 86, 89, 11]
```

To solve this, Python provides *generator expressions*, a generalization of list comprehensions and generators. Generator expressions don't materialize the whole output sequence when they're run. Instead, generator expressions evaluate to an iterator that yields one item at a time from the expression.

A generator expression is created by putting list-comprehension-like syntax between () characters. Here, I use a generator expression that is equivalent to the code above. However, the generator expression immediately evaluates to an iterator and doesn't make any forward progress.

```
it = (len(x) for x in open('/tmp/my_file.txt'))
print(it)

>>>
<generator object <genexpr> at 0x101b81480>
```

The returned iterator can be advanced one step at a time to produce the next output from the generator expression as needed (using the `next` built-in function). Your code can consume as much of the generator expression as you want without risking a blowup in memory usage.

```
print(next(it))
print(next(it))

>>>
100
57
```

Another powerful outcome of generator expressions is that they can be composed together. Here, I take the iterator returned by the generator expression above and use it as the input for another generator expression.

```
roots = ((x, x**0.5) for x in it)
```

Each time I advance this iterator, it will also advance the interior iterator, creating a domino effect of looping, evaluating conditional expressions, and passing around inputs and outputs.

```
print(next(roots))

>>>
(15, 3.872983346207417)
```

Chaining generators like this executes very quickly in Python. When you're looking for a way to compose functionality that's operating on a large stream of input, generator expressions are the best tool for the job. The only gotcha is that the iterators returned by generator expressions are stateful, so you must be careful not to use them more than once (see Item 17: "Be Defensive When Iterating Over Arguments").

### Things to Remember

- ✦ List comprehensions can cause problems for large inputs by using too much memory.
- ✦ Generator expressions avoid memory issues by producing outputs one at a time as an iterator.
- ✦ Generator expressions can be composed by passing the iterator from one generator expression into the `for` subexpression of another.
- ✦ Generator expressions execute very quickly when chained together.

## Item 10: Prefer enumerate Over range

The `range` built-in function is useful for loops that iterate over a set of integers.

```
random_bits = 0
for i in range(64):
    if randint(0, 1):
        random_bits |= 1 << i
```

When you have a data structure to iterate over, like a list of strings, you can loop directly over the sequence.

```
flavor_list = ['vanilla', 'chocolate', 'pecan', 'strawberry']
for flavor in flavor_list:
    print('%s is delicious' % flavor)
```

Often, you'll want to iterate over a list and also know the index of the current item in the list. For example, say you want to print the ranking of your favorite ice cream flavors. One way to do it is using `range`.

```
for i in range(len(flavor_list)):
    flavor = flavor_list[i]
    print('%d: %s' % (i + 1, flavor))
```

This looks clumsy compared with the other examples of iterating over `flavor_list` or `range`. You have to get the length of the list. You have to index into the array. It's harder to read.

Python provides the `enumerate` built-in function for addressing this situation. `enumerate` wraps any iterator with a lazy generator. This generator yields pairs of the loop index and the next value from the iterator. The resulting code is much clearer.

```
for i, flavor in enumerate(flavor_list):
    print('%d: %s' % (i + 1, flavor))
```

```
>>>
1: vanilla
2: chocolate
3: pecan
4: strawberry
```

You can make this even shorter by specifying the number from which enumerate should begin counting (1 in this case).

```
for i, flavor in enumerate(flavor_list, 1):
    print('%d: %s' % (i, flavor))
```

### Things to Remember

- ✦ enumerate provides concise syntax for looping over an iterator and getting the index of each item from the iterator as you go.
- ✦ Prefer enumerate instead of looping over a range and indexing into a sequence.
- ✦ You can supply a second parameter to enumerate to specify the number from which to begin counting (zero is the default).

## Item 11: Use zip to Process Iterators in Parallel

Often in Python you find yourself with many lists of related objects. List comprehensions make it easy to take a source list and get a derived list by applying an expression (see Item 7: "Use List Comprehensions Instead of map and filter").

```
names = ['Cecilia', 'Lise', 'Marie']
letters = [len(n) for n in names]
```

The items in the derived list are related to the items in the source list by their indexes. To iterate over both lists in parallel, you can iterate over the length of the names source list.

```
longest_name = None
max_letters = 0

for i in range(len(names)):
    count = letters[i]
    if count > max_letters:
        longest_name = names[i]
        max_letters = count

print(longest_name)

>>>
Cecilia
```

The problem is that this whole loop statement is visually noisy. The indexes into names and letters make the code hard to read. Indexing into the arrays by the loop index i happens twice. Using enumerate (see Item 10: "Prefer enumerate Over range") improves this slightly, but it's still not ideal.

```
for i, name in enumerate(names):
    count = letters[i]
    if count > max_letters:
        longest_name = name
        max_letters = count
```

To make this code clearer, Python provides the zip built-in function. In Python 3, zip wraps two or more iterators with a lazy generator. The zip generator yields tuples containing the next value from each iterator. The resulting code is much cleaner than indexing into multiple lists.

```
for name, count in zip(names, letters):
    if count > max_letters:
        longest_name = name
        max_letters = count
```

There are two problems with the zip built-in.

The first issue is that in Python 2 zip is not a generator; it will fully exhaust the supplied iterators and return a list of all the tuples it creates. This could potentially use a lot of memory and cause your program to crash. If you want to zip very large iterators in Python 2, you should use izip from the itertools built-in module (see Item 46: "Use Built-in Algorithms and Data Structures").

The second issue is that zip behaves strangely if the input iterators are of different lengths. For example, say you add another name to the list above but forget to update the letter counts. Running zip on the two input lists will have an unexpected result.

```
names.append('Rosalind')
for name, count in zip(names, letters):
    print(name)

>>>
Cecilia
Lise
Marie
```

The new item for 'Rosalind' isn't there. This is just how zip works. It keeps yielding tuples until a wrapped iterator is exhausted. This approach works fine when you know that the iterators are of the same length, which is often the case for derived lists created by list comprehensions. In many other cases, the truncating behavior of zip is surprising and bad. If you aren't confident that the lengths of the lists you want to zip are equal, consider using the zip_longest function from the itertools built-in module instead (also called izip_longest in Python 2).

**Things to Remember**

- ✦ The zip built-in function can be used to iterate over multiple iterators in parallel.
- ✦ In Python 3, zip is a lazy generator that produces tuples. In Python 2, zip returns the full result as a list of tuples.
- ✦ zip truncates its output silently if you supply it with iterators of different lengths.
- ✦ The zip_longest function from the itertools built-in module lets you iterate over multiple iterators in parallel regardless of their lengths (see Item 46: "Use Built-in Algorithms and Data Structures").

## Item 12: Avoid else Blocks After for and while Loops

Python loops have an extra feature that is not available in most other programming languages: you can put an else block immediately after a loop's repeated interior block.

```
for i in range(3):
    print('Loop %d' % i)
else:
    print('Else block!')

>>>
Loop 0
Loop 1
Loop 2
Else block!
```

Surprisingly, the else block runs immediately after the loop finishes. Why is the clause called "else"? Why not "and"? In an if/else statement, else means, "Do this if the block before this doesn't happen." In a try/except statement, except has the same definition: "Do this if trying the block before this failed."

Similarly, else from try/except/else follows this pattern (see Item 13: "Take Advantage of Each Block in try/except/else/finally") because it means, "Do this if the block before did not fail." try/finally is also intuitive because it means, "Always do what is final after trying the block before."

Given all of the uses of else, except, and finally in Python, a new programmer might assume that the else part of for/else means, "Do this if the loop wasn't completed." In reality, it does exactly the opposite. Using a break statement in a loop will actually skip the else block.

```
for i in range(3):
    print('Loop %d' % i)
    if i == 1:
        break
else:
    print('Else block!')

>>>
Loop 0
Loop 1
```

Another surprise is that the else block will run immediately if you loop over an empty sequence.

```
for x in []:
    print('Never runs')
else:
    print('For Else block!')

>>>
For Else block!
```

The else block also runs when while loops are initially false.

```
while False:
    print('Never runs')
else:
    print('While Else block!')

>>>
While Else block!
```

The rationale for these behaviors is that else blocks after loops are useful when you're using loops to search for something. For example, say you want to determine whether two numbers are coprime (their only common divisor is 1). Here, I iterate through every possible common divisor and test the numbers. After every option has been tried, the loop ends. The else block runs when the numbers are coprime because the loop doesn't encounter a break.

```
a = 4
b = 9
for i in range(2, min(a, b) + 1):
    print('Testing', i)
    if a % i == 0 and b % i == 0:
        print('Not coprime')
        break
else:
    print('Coprime')
```

```
>>>
Testing 2
Testing 3
Testing 4
Coprime
```

In practice, you wouldn't write the code this way. Instead, you'd write a helper function to do the calculation. Such a helper function is written in two common styles.

The first approach is to return early when you find the condition you're looking for. You return the default outcome if you fall through the loop.

```
def coprime(a, b):
    for i in range(2, min(a, b) + 1):
        if a % i == 0 and b % i == 0:
            return False
    return True
```

The second way is to have a result variable that indicates whether you've found what you're looking for in the loop. You `break` out of the loop as soon as you find something.

```
def coprime2(a, b):
    is_coprime = True
    for i in range(2, min(a, b) + 1):
        if a % i == 0 and b % i == 0:
            is_coprime = False
            break
    return is_coprime
```

Both of these approaches are so much clearer to readers of unfamiliar code. The expressivity you gain from the `else` block doesn't outweigh the burden you put on people (including yourself) who want to understand your code in the future. Simple constructs like loops should be self-evident in Python. You should avoid using `else` blocks after loops entirely.

### Things to Remember

- ✦ Python has special syntax that allows `else` blocks to immediately follow `for` and `while` loop interior blocks.
- ✦ The `else` block after a loop only runs if the loop body did not encounter a `break` statement.
- ✦ Avoid using `else` blocks after loops because their behavior isn't intuitive and can be confusing.

## Item 13: Take Advantage of Each Block in `try/except/else/finally`

There are four distinct times that you may want to take action during exception handling in Python. These are captured in the functionality of `try`, `except`, `else`, and `finally` blocks. Each block serves a unique purpose in the compound statement, and their various combinations are useful (see Item 51: "Define a Root `Exception` to Insulate Callers from APIs" for another example).

### Finally Blocks

Use `try/finally` when you want exceptions to propagate up, but you also want to run cleanup code even when exceptions occur. One common usage of `try/finally` is for reliably closing file handles (see Item 43: "Consider `contextlib` and `with` Statements for Reusable `try/finally` Behavior" for another approach).

```
handle = open('/tmp/random_data.txt')  # May raise IOError
try:
    data = handle.read()  # May raise UnicodeDecodeError
finally:
    handle.close()        # Always runs after try:
```

Any exception raised by the `read` method will always propagate up to the calling code, yet the `close` method of `handle` is also guaranteed to run in the `finally` block. You must call `open` before the `try` block because exceptions that occur when opening the file (like `IOError` if the file does not exist) should skip the `finally` block.

### Else Blocks

Use `try/except/else` to make it clear which exceptions will be handled by your code and which exceptions will propagate up. When the `try` block doesn't raise an exception, the `else` block will run. The `else` block helps you minimize the amount of code in the `try` block and improves readability. For example, say you want to load JSON dictionary data from a string and return the value of a key it contains.

```
def load_json_key(data, key):
    try:
        result_dict = json.loads(data)  # May raise ValueError
    except ValueError as e:
        raise KeyError from e
    else:
        return result_dict[key]         # May raise KeyError
```

If the data isn't valid JSON, then decoding with `json.loads` will raise a `ValueError`. The exception is caught by the `except` block and handled. If decoding is successful, then the key lookup will occur in the `else` block. If the key lookup raises any exceptions, they will propagate up to the caller because they are outside the `try` block. The `else` clause ensures that what follows the `try/except` is visually distinguished from the `except` block. This makes the exception propagation behavior clear.

### Everything Together

Use `try/except/else/finally` when you want to do it all in one compound statement. For example, say you want to read a description of work to do from a file, process it, and then update the file in place. Here, the `try` block is used to read the file and process it. The `except` block is used to handle exceptions from the `try` block that are expected. The `else` block is used to update the file in place and to allow related exceptions to propagate up. The `finally` block cleans up the file handle.

```
UNDEFINED = object()

def divide_json(path):
    handle = open(path, 'r+')   # May raise IOError
    try:
        data = handle.read()    # May raise UnicodeDecodeError
        op = json.loads(data)   # May raise ValueError
        value = (
            op['numerator'] /
            op['denominator'])  # May raise ZeroDivisionError
    except ZeroDivisionError as e:
        return UNDEFINED
    else:
        op['result'] = value
        result = json.dumps(op)
        handle.seek(0)
        handle.write(result)    # May raise IOError
        return value
    finally:
        handle.close()          # Always runs
```

This layout is especially useful because all of the blocks work together in intuitive ways. For example, if an exception gets raised in the `else` block while rewriting the result data, the `finally` block will still run and close the file handle.

### Things to Remember

- ✦ The `try`/`finally` compound statement lets you run cleanup code regardless of whether exceptions were raised in the `try` block.
- ✦ The `else` block helps you minimize the amount of code in `try` blocks and visually distinguish the success case from the `try`/`except` blocks.
- ✦ An `else` block can be used to perform additional actions after a successful `try` block but before common cleanup in a `finally` block.

# 2 Functions

The first organizational tool programmers use in Python is the *function*. As in other programming languages, functions enable you to break large programs into smaller, simpler pieces. They improve readability and make code more approachable. They allow for reuse and refactoring.

Functions in Python have a variety of extra features that make the programmer's life easier. Some are similar to capabilities in other programming languages, but many are unique to Python. These extras can make a function's purpose more obvious. They can eliminate noise and clarify the intention of callers. They can significantly reduce subtle bugs that are difficult to find.

## Item 14: Prefer Exceptions to Returning `None`

When writing utility functions, there's a draw for Python programmers to give special meaning to the return value of `None`. It seems to makes sense in some cases. For example, say you want a helper function that divides one number by another. In the case of dividing by zero, returning `None` seems natural because the result is undefined.

```
def divide(a, b):
    try:
        return a / b
    except ZeroDivisionError:
        return None
```

Code using this function can interpret the return value accordingly.

```
result = divide(x, y)
if result is None:
    print('Invalid inputs')
```

What happens when the numerator is zero? That will cause the return value to also be zero (if the denominator is non-zero). This can cause problems when you evaluate the result in a condition like an `if` statement. You may accidentally look for any `False` equivalent value to indicate errors instead of only looking for `None` (see Item 4: "Write Helper Functions Instead of Complex Expressions" for a similar situation).

```
x, y = 0, 5
result = divide(x, y)
if not result:
    print('Invalid inputs')  # This is wrong!
```

This is a common mistake in Python code when `None` has special meaning. This is why returning `None` from a function is error prone. There are two ways to reduce the chance of such errors.

The first way is to split the return value into a two-tuple. The first part of the tuple indicates that the operation was a success or failure. The second part is the actual result that was computed.

```
def divide(a, b):
    try:
        return True, a / b
    except ZeroDivisionError:
        return False, None
```

Callers of this function have to unpack the tuple. That forces them to consider the status part of the tuple instead of just looking at the result of division.

```
success, result = divide(x, y)
if not success:
    print('Invalid inputs')
```

The problem is that callers can easily ignore the first part of the tuple (using the underscore variable name, a Python convention for unused variables). The resulting code doesn't look wrong at first glance. This is as bad as just returning `None`.

```
_, result = divide(x, y)
if not result:
    print('Invalid inputs')
```

The second, better way to reduce these errors is to never return `None` at all. Instead, raise an exception up to the caller and make them deal with it. Here, I turn a `ZeroDivisionError` into a `ValueError` to indicate to the caller that the input values are bad:

```
def divide(a, b):
    try:
        return a / b
    except ZeroDivisionError as e:
        raise ValueError('Invalid inputs') from e
```

Now the caller should handle the exception for the invalid input case (this behavior should be documented; see Item 49: "Write Docstrings for Every Function, Class, and Module"). The caller no longer requires a condition on the return value of the function. If the function didn't raise an exception, then the return value must be good. The outcome of exception handling is clear.

```
x, y = 5, 2
try:
    result = divide(x, y)
except ValueError:
    print('Invalid inputs')
else:
    print('Result is %.1f' % result)

>>>
Result is 2.5
```

### Things to Remember

- ✦ Functions that return `None` to indicate special meaning are error prone because `None` and other values (e.g., zero, the empty string) all evaluate to `False` in conditional expressions.
- ✦ Raise exceptions to indicate special situations instead of returning `None`. Expect the calling code to handle exceptions properly when they're documented.

## Item 15: Know How Closures Interact with Variable Scope

Say you want to sort a list of numbers but prioritize one group of numbers to come first. This pattern is useful when you're rendering a user interface and want important messages or exceptional events to be displayed before everything else.

A common way to do this is to pass a helper function as the `key` argument to a list's `sort` method. The helper's return value will be used as the value for sorting each item in the list. The helper can check whether the given item is in the important group and can vary the sort key accordingly.

```
def sort_priority(values, group):
    def helper(x):
        if x in group:
            return (0, x)
        return (1, x)
    values.sort(key=helper)
```

This function works for simple inputs.

```
numbers = [8, 3, 1, 2, 5, 4, 7, 6]
group = {2, 3, 5, 7}
sort_priority(numbers, group)
print(numbers)

>>>
[2, 3, 5, 7, 1, 4, 6, 8]
```

There are three reasons why this function operates as expected:

- Python supports *closures*: functions that refer to variables from the scope in which they were defined. This is why the `helper` function is able to access the `group` argument to `sort_priority`.
- Functions are *first-class* objects in Python, meaning you can refer to them directly, assign them to variables, pass them as arguments to other functions, compare them in expressions and `if` statements, etc. This is how the `sort` method can accept a closure function as the `key` argument.
- Python has specific rules for comparing tuples. It first compares items in index zero, then index one, then index two, and so on. This is why the return value from the `helper` closure causes the sort order to have two distinct groups.

It'd be nice if this function returned whether higher-priority items were seen at all so the user interface code can act accordingly. Adding such behavior seems straightforward. There's already a closure function for deciding which group each number is in. Why not also use the closure to flip a flag when high-priority items are seen? Then the function can return the flag value after it's been modified by the closure.

Here, I try to do that in a seemingly obvious way:

```
def sort_priority2(numbers, group):
    found = False
    def helper(x):
        if x in group:
            found = True  # Seems simple
```

```
            return (0, x)
        return (1, x)
    numbers.sort(key=helper)
    return found
```

I can run the function on the same inputs as before.

```
found = sort_priority2(numbers, group)
print('Found:', found)
print(numbers)

>>>
Found: False
[2, 3, 5, 7, 1, 4, 6, 8]
```

The sorted results are correct, but the `found` result is wrong. Items from `group` were definitely found in `numbers`, but the function returned `False`. How could this happen?

When you reference a variable in an expression, the Python interpreter will traverse the scope to resolve the reference in this order:

1. The current function's scope
2. Any enclosing scopes (like other containing functions)
3. The scope of the module that contains the code (also called the *global scope*)
4. The built-in scope (that contains functions like `len` and `str`)

If none of these places have a defined variable with the referenced name, then a `NameError` exception is raised.

Assigning a value to a variable works differently. If the variable is already defined in the current scope, then it will just take on the new value. If the variable doesn't exist in the current scope, then Python treats the assignment as a variable definition. The scope of the newly defined variable is the function that contains the assignment.

This assignment behavior explains the wrong return value of the `sort_priority2` function. The `found` variable is assigned to `True` in the `helper` closure. The closure's assignment is treated as a new variable definition within `helper`, not as an assignment within `sort_priority2`.

```
def sort_priority2(numbers, group):
    found = False         # Scope: 'sort_priority2'
    def helper(x):
        if x in group:
            found = True  # Scope: 'helper' -- Bad!
            return (0, x)
```

```
        return (1, x)
    numbers.sort(key=helper)
    return found
```

Encountering this problem is sometimes called the *scoping bug* because it can be so surprising to newbies. But this is the intended result. This behavior prevents local variables in a function from polluting the containing module. Otherwise, every assignment within a function would put garbage into the global module scope. Not only would that be noise, but the interplay of the resulting global variables could cause obscure bugs.

### Getting Data Out

In Python 3, there is special syntax for getting data out of a closure. The `nonlocal` statement is used to indicate that scope traversal should happen upon assignment for a specific variable name. The only limit is that `nonlocal` won't traverse up to the module-level scope (to avoid polluting globals).

Here, I define the same function again using `nonlocal`:

```
def sort_priority3(numbers, group):
    found = False
    def helper(x):
        nonlocal found
        if x in group:
            found = True
            return (0, x)
        return (1, x)
    numbers.sort(key=helper)
    return found
```

The `nonlocal` statement makes it clear when data is being assigned out of a closure into another scope. It's complementary to the `global` statement, which indicates that a variable's assignment should go directly into the module scope.

However, much like the anti-pattern of global variables, I'd caution against using `nonlocal` for anything beyond simple functions. The side effects of `nonlocal` can be hard to follow. It's especially hard to understand in long functions where the `nonlocal` statements and assignments to associated variables are far apart.

When your usage of `nonlocal` starts getting complicated, it's better to wrap your state in a helper class. Here, I define a class that achieves the same result as the `nonlocal` approach. It's a little longer, but is much easier to read (see Item 23: "Accept Functions for Simple Interfaces Instead of Classes" for details on the `__call__` special method).

```
class Sorter(object):
    def __init__(self, group):
        self.group = group
        self.found = False

    def __call__(self, x):
        if x in self.group:
            self.found = True
            return (0, x)
        return (1, x)

sorter = Sorter(group)
numbers.sort(key=sorter)
assert sorter.found is True
```

### Scope in Python 2

Unfortunately, Python 2 doesn't support the `nonlocal` keyword. In order to get similar behavior, you need to use a work-around that takes advantage of Python's scoping rules. This approach isn't pretty, but it's the common Python idiom.

```
# Python 2
def sort_priority(numbers, group):
    found = [False]
    def helper(x):
        if x in group:
            found[0] = True
            return (0, x)
        return (1, x)
    numbers.sort(key=helper)
    return found[0]
```

As explained above, Python will traverse up the scope where the `found` variable is referenced to resolve its current value. The trick is that the value for `found` is a list, which is mutable. This means that once retrieved, the closure can modify the state of `found` to send data out of the inner scope (with `found[0] = True`).

This approach also works when the variable used to traverse the scope is a dictionary, a set, or an instance of a class you've defined.

### Things to Remember

- ✦ Closure functions can refer to variables from any of the scopes in which they were defined.
- ✦ By default, closures can't affect enclosing scopes by assigning variables.
- ✦ In Python 3, use the nonlocal statement to indicate when a closure can modify a variable in its enclosing scopes.
- ✦ In Python 2, use a mutable value (like a single-item list) to work around the lack of the nonlocal statement.
- ✦ Avoid using nonlocal statements for anything beyond simple functions.

## Item 16: Consider Generators Instead of Returning Lists

The simplest choice for functions that produce a sequence of results is to return a list of items. For example, say you want to find the index of every word in a string. Here, I accumulate results in a list using the append method and return it at the end of the function:

```
def index_words(text):
    result = []
    if text:
        result.append(0)
    for index, letter in enumerate(text):
        if letter == ' ':
            result.append(index + 1)
    return result
```

This works as expected for some sample input.

```
address = 'Four score and seven years ago...'
result = index_words(address)
print(result[:3])

>>>
[0, 5, 11]
```

There are two problems with the index_words function.

The first problem is that the code is a bit dense and noisy. Each time a new result is found, I call the append method. The method call's bulk (result.append) deemphasizes the value being added to the list (index + 1). There is one line for creating the result list and another for returning it. While the function body contains ~130 characters (without whitespace), only ~75 characters are important.

A better way to write this function is using a *generator*. Generators are functions that use `yield` expressions. When called, generator functions do not actually run but instead immediately return an iterator. With each call to the `next` built-in function, the iterator will advance the generator to its next `yield` expression. Each value passed to `yield` by the generator will be returned by the iterator to the caller.

Here, I define a generator function that produces the same results as before:

```
def index_words_iter(text):
    if text:
        yield 0
    for index, letter in enumerate(text):
        if letter == ' ':
            yield index + 1
```

It's significantly easier to read because all interactions with the result list have been eliminated. Results are passed to `yield` expressions instead. The iterator returned by the generator call can easily be converted to a list by passing it to the `list` built-in function (see Item 9: "Consider Generator Expressions for Large Comprehensions" for how this works).

```
result = list(index_words_iter(address))
```

The second problem with `index_words` is that it requires all results to be stored in the list before being returned. For huge inputs, this can cause your program to run out of memory and crash. In contrast, a generator version of this function can easily be adapted to take inputs of arbitrary length.

Here, I define a generator that streams input from a file one line at a time and yields outputs one word at a time. The working memory for this function is bounded to the maximum length of one line of input.

```
def index_file(handle):
    offset = 0
    for line in handle:
        if line:
            yield offset
        for letter in line:
            offset += 1
            if letter == ' ':
                yield offset
```

Running the generator produces the same results.

```
with open('/tmp/address.txt', 'r') as f:
    it = index_file(f)
    results = islice(it, 0, 3)
    print(list(results))

>>>
[0, 5, 11]
```

The only gotcha of defining generators like this is that the callers must be aware that the iterators returned are stateful and can't be reused (see Item 17: "Be Defensive When Iterating Over Arguments").

### Things to Remember

- ✦ Using generators can be clearer than the alternative of returning lists of accumulated results.
- ✦ The iterator returned by a generator produces the set of values passed to `yield` expressions within the generator function's body.
- ✦ Generators can produce a sequence of outputs for arbitrarily large inputs because their working memory doesn't include all inputs and outputs.

## Item 17: Be Defensive When Iterating Over Arguments

When a function takes a list of objects as a parameter, it's often important to iterate over that list multiple times. For example, say you want to analyze tourism numbers for the U.S. state of Texas. Imagine the data set is the number of visitors to each city (in millions per year). You'd like to figure out what percentage of overall tourism each city receives.

To do this you need a normalization function. It sums the inputs to determine the total number of tourists per year. Then it divides each city's individual visitor count by the total to find that city's contribution to the whole.

```
def normalize(numbers):
    total = sum(numbers)
    result = []
    for value in numbers:
        percent = 100 * value / total
        result.append(percent)
    return result
```

This function works when given a list of visits.

```
visits = [15, 35, 80]
percentages = normalize(visits)
print(percentages)

>>>
[11.538461538461538, 26.923076923076923, 61.53846153846154]
```

To scale this up, I need to read the data from a file that contains every city in all of Texas. I define a generator to do this because then I can reuse the same function later when I want to compute tourism numbers for the whole world, a much larger data set (see Item 16: "Consider Generators Instead of Returning Lists").

```
def read_visits(data_path):
    with open(data_path) as f:
        for line in f:
            yield int(line)
```

Surprisingly, calling `normalize` on the generator's return value produces no results.

```
it = read_visits('/tmp/my_numbers.txt')
percentages = normalize(it)
print(percentages)

>>>
[]
```

The cause of this behavior is that an iterator only produces its results a single time. If you iterate over an iterator or generator that has already raised a `StopIteration` exception, you won't get any results the second time around.

```
it = read_visits('/tmp/my_numbers.txt')
print(list(it))
print(list(it))  # Already exhausted

>>>
[15, 35, 80]
[]
```

What's confusing is that you also won't get any errors when you iterate over an already exhausted iterator. `for` loops, the `list` constructor, and many other functions throughout the Python standard library expect the `StopIteration` exception to be raised during normal operation. These functions can't tell the difference between an iterator that has no output and an iterator that had output and is now exhausted.

To solve this problem, you can explicitly exhaust an input iterator and keep a copy of its entire contents in a list. You can then iterate over the list version of the data as many times as you need to. Here's the same function as before, but it defensively copies the input iterator:

```
def normalize_copy(numbers):
    numbers = list(numbers)  # Copy the iterator
    total = sum(numbers)
    result = []
    for value in numbers:
        percent = 100 * value / total
        result.append(percent)
    return result
```

Now the function works correctly on a generator's return value.

```
it = read_visits('/tmp/my_numbers.txt')
percentages = normalize_copy(it)
print(percentages)

>>>
[11.538461538461538, 26.923076923076923, 61.53846153846154]
```

The problem with this approach is the copy of the input iterator's contents could be large. Copying the iterator could cause your program to run out of memory and crash. One way around this is to accept a function that returns a new iterator each time it's called.

```
def normalize_func(get_iter):
    total = sum(get_iter())   # New iterator
    result = []
    for value in get_iter():  # New iterator
        percent = 100 * value / total
        result.append(percent)
    return result
```

To use `normalize_func`, you can pass in a `lambda` expression that calls the generator and produces a new iterator each time.

```
percentages = normalize_func(lambda: read_visits(path))
```

Though it works, having to pass a lambda function like this is clumsy. The better way to achieve the same result is to provide a new container class that implements the *iterator protocol*.

The iterator protocol is how Python `for` loops and related expressions traverse the contents of a container type. When Python sees a statement like for x in foo it will actually call iter(foo). The iter built-in function calls the foo.__iter__ special method in turn. The __iter__ method must return an iterator object (which itself implements the __next__ special method). Then the for loop repeatedly calls the next built-in function on the iterator object until it's exhausted (and raises a StopIteration exception).

It sounds complicated, but practically speaking you can achieve all of this behavior for your classes by implementing the __iter__ method as a generator. Here, I define an iterable container class that reads the files containing tourism data:

```
class ReadVisits(object):
    def __init__(self, data_path):
        self.data_path = data_path

    def __iter__(self):
        with open(self.data_path) as f:
            for line in f:
                yield int(line)
```

This new container type works correctly when passed to the original function without any modifications.

```
visits = ReadVisits(path)
percentages = normalize(visits)
print(percentages)

>>>
[11.538461538461538, 26.923076923076923, 61.53846153846154]
```

This works because the sum method in normalize will call ReadVisits.__iter__ to allocate a new iterator object. The for loop to normalize the numbers will also call __iter__ to allocate a second iterator object. Each of those iterators will be advanced and exhausted independently, ensuring that each unique iteration sees all of the input data values. The only downside of this approach is that it reads the input data multiple times.

Now that you know how containers like ReadVisits work, you can write your functions to ensure that parameters aren't just iterators. The protocol states that when an iterator is passed to the iter built-in function, iter will return the iterator itself. In contrast, when a container type is passed to iter, a new iterator object will be returned each time. Thus, you can test an input value for this behavior and raise a TypeError to reject iterators.

```
def normalize_defensive(numbers):
    if iter(numbers) is iter(numbers):  # An iterator -- bad!
        raise TypeError('Must supply a container')
    total = sum(numbers)
    result = []
    for value in numbers:
        percent = 100 * value / total
        result.append(percent)
    return result
```

This is ideal if you don't want to copy the full input iterator like `normalize_copy` above, but you also need to iterate over the input data multiple times. This function works as expected for `list` and `ReadVisits` inputs because they are containers. It will work for any type of container that follows the iterator protocol.

```
visits = [15, 35, 80]
normalize_defensive(visits)  # No error
visits = ReadVisits(path)
normalize_defensive(visits)  # No error
```

The function will raise an exception if the input is iterable but not a container.

```
it = iter(visits)
normalize_defensive(it)

>>>
TypeError: Must supply a container
```

### Things to Remember

- ✦ Beware of functions that iterate over input arguments multiple times. If these arguments are iterators, you may see strange behavior and missing values.
- ✦ Python's iterator protocol defines how containers and iterators interact with the `iter` and `next` built-in functions, `for` loops, and related expressions.
- ✦ You can easily define your own iterable container type by implementing the `__iter__` method as a generator.
- ✦ You can detect that a value is an iterator (instead of a container) if calling `iter` on it twice produces the same result, which can then be progressed with the `next` built-in function.

## Item 18: Reduce Visual Noise with Variable Positional Arguments

Accepting optional positional arguments (often called *star args* in reference to the conventional name for the parameter, *args) can make a function call more clear and remove *visual noise*.

For example, say you want to log some debug information. With a fixed number of arguments, you would need a function that takes a message and a list of values.

```
def log(message, values):
    if not values:
        print(message)
    else:
        values_str = ', '.join(str(x) for x in values)
        print('%s: %s' % (message, values_str))

log('My numbers are', [1, 2])
log('Hi there', [])

>>>
My numbers are: 1, 2
Hi there
```

Having to pass an empty list when you have no values to log is cumbersome and noisy. It'd be better to leave out the second argument entirely. You can do this in Python by prefixing the last positional parameter name with *. The first parameter for the log message is required, whereas any number of subsequent positional arguments are optional. The function body doesn't need to change, only the callers do.

```
def log(message, *values):  # The only difference
    if not values:
        print(message)
    else:
        values_str = ', '.join(str(x) for x in values)
        print('%s: %s' % (message, values_str))

log('My numbers are', 1, 2)
log('Hi there')  # Much better

>>>
My numbers are: 1, 2
Hi there
```

If you already have a list and want to call a variable argument function like log, you can do this by using the * operator. This instructs Python to pass items from the sequence as positional arguments.

```
favorites = [7, 33, 99]
log('Favorite colors', *favorites)

>>>
Favorite colors: 7, 33, 99
```

There are two problems with accepting a variable number of positional arguments.

The first issue is that the variable arguments are always turned into a tuple before they are passed to your function. This means that if the caller of your function uses the * operator on a generator, it will be iterated until it's exhausted. The resulting tuple will include every value from the generator, which could consume a lot of memory and cause your program to crash.

```
def my_generator():
    for i in range(10):
        yield i

def my_func(*args):
    print(args)

it = my_generator()
my_func(*it)

>>>
(0, 1, 2, 3, 4, 5, 6, 7, 8, 9)
```

Functions that accept *args are best for situations where you know the number of inputs in the argument list will be reasonably small. It's ideal for function calls that pass many literals or variable names together. It's primarily for the convenience of the programmer and the readability of the code.

The second issue with *args is that you can't add new positional arguments to your function in the future without migrating every caller. If you try to add a positional argument in the front of the argument list, existing callers will subtly break if they aren't updated.

```
def log(sequence, message, *values):
    if not values:
        print('%s: %s' % (sequence, message))
    else:
        values_str = ', '.join(str(x) for x in values)
        print('%s: %s: %s' % (sequence, message, values_str))
```

```
log(1, 'Favorites', 7, 33)      # New usage is OK
log('Favorite numbers', 7, 33)  # Old usage breaks

>>>
1: Favorites: 7, 33
Favorite numbers: 7: 33
```

The problem here is that the second call to `log` used `7` as the `message` parameter because a `sequence` argument wasn't given. Bugs like this are hard to track down because the code still runs without raising any exceptions. To avoid this possibility entirely, you should use keyword-only arguments when you want to extend functions that accept `*args` (see Item 21: "Enforce Clarity with Keyword-Only Arguments").

### Things to Remember

- Functions can accept a variable number of positional arguments by using `*args` in the `def` statement.
- You can use the items from a sequence as the positional arguments for a function with the `*` operator.
- Using the `*` operator with a generator may cause your program to run out of memory and crash.
- Adding new positional parameters to functions that accept `*args` can introduce hard-to-find bugs.

## Item 19: Provide Optional Behavior with Keyword Arguments

Like most other programming languages, calling a function in Python allows for passing arguments by position.

```
def remainder(number, divisor):
    return number % divisor

assert remainder(20, 7) == 6
```

All positional arguments to Python functions can also be passed by keyword, where the name of the argument is used in an assignment within the parentheses of a function call. The keyword arguments can be passed in any order as long as all of the required positional arguments are specified. You can mix and match keyword and positional arguments. These calls are equivalent:

```
remainder(20, 7)
remainder(20, divisor=7)
remainder(number=20, divisor=7)
remainder(divisor=7, number=20)
```

Positional arguments must be specified before keyword arguments.

```
remainder(number=20, 7)

>>>
SyntaxError: non-keyword arg after keyword arg
```

Each argument can only be specified once.

```
remainder(20, number=7)

>>>
TypeError: remainder() got multiple values for argument
➥'number'
```

The flexibility of keyword arguments provides three significant benefits.

The first advantage is that keyword arguments make the function call clearer to new readers of the code. With the call `remainder(20, 7)`, it's not evident which argument is the number and which is the divisor without looking at the implementation of the `remainder` method. In the call with keyword arguments, `number=20` and `divisor=7` make it immediately obvious which parameter is being used for each purpose.

The second impact of keyword arguments is that they can have default values specified in the function definition. This allows a function to provide additional capabilities when you need them but lets you accept the default behavior most of the time. This can eliminate repetitive code and reduce noise.

For example, say you want to compute the rate of fluid flowing into a vat. If the vat is also on a scale, then you could use the difference between two weight measurements at two different times to determine the flow rate.

```
def flow_rate(weight_diff, time_diff):
    return weight_diff / time_diff

weight_diff = 0.5
time_diff = 3
flow = flow_rate(weight_diff, time_diff)
print('%.3f kg per second' % flow)

>>>
0.167 kg per second
```

In the typical case, it's useful to know the flow rate in kilograms per second. Other times, it'd be helpful to use the last sensor measurements to approximate larger time scales, like hours or days. You can provide this behavior in the same function by adding an argument for the time period scaling factor.

```
def flow_rate(weight_diff, time_diff, period):
    return (weight_diff / time_diff) * period
```

The problem is that now you need to specify the period argument every time you call the function, even in the common case of flow rate per second (where the period is 1).

```
flow_per_second = flow_rate(weight_diff, time_diff, 1)
```

To make this less noisy, I can give the period argument a default value.

```
def flow_rate(weight_diff, time_diff, period=1):
    return (weight_diff / time_diff) * period
```

The period argument is now optional.

```
flow_per_second = flow_rate(weight_diff, time_diff)
flow_per_hour = flow_rate(weight_diff, time_diff, period=3600)
```

This works well for simple default values (it gets tricky for complex default values—see Item 20: "Use None and Docstrings to Specify Dynamic Default Arguments").

The third reason to use keyword arguments is that they provide a powerful way to extend a function's parameters while remaining backwards compatible with existing callers. This lets you provide additional functionality without having to migrate a lot of code, reducing the chance of introducing bugs.

For example, say you want to extend the flow_rate function above to calculate flow rates in weight units besides kilograms. You can do this by adding a new optional parameter that provides a conversion rate to your preferred measurement units.

```
def flow_rate(weight_diff, time_diff,
              period=1, units_per_kg=1):
    return ((weight_diff / units_per_kg) / time_diff) * period
```

The default argument value for units_per_kg is 1, which makes the returned weight units remain as kilograms. This means that all existing callers will see no change in behavior. New callers to flow_rate can specify the new keyword argument to see the new behavior.

```
pounds_per_hour = flow_rate(weight_diff, time_diff,
                            period=3600, units_per_kg=2.2)
```

The only problem with this approach is that optional keyword arguments like period and units_per_kg may still be specified as positional arguments.

```
pounds_per_hour = flow_rate(weight_diff, time_diff, 3600, 2.2)
```

Supplying optional arguments positionally can be confusing because it isn't clear what the values 3600 and 2.2 correspond to. The best practice is to always specify optional arguments using the keyword names and never pass them as positional arguments.

> **Note**
> Backwards compatibility using optional keyword arguments like this is crucial for functions that accept *args (see Item 18: "Reduce Visual Noise with Variable Positional Arguments"). But an even better practice is to use keyword-only arguments (see Item 21: "Enforce Clarity with Keyword-Only Arguments").

### Things to Remember

- ✦ Function arguments can be specified by position or by keyword.
- ✦ Keywords make it clear what the purpose of each argument is when it would be confusing with only positional arguments.
- ✦ Keyword arguments with default values make it easy to add new behaviors to a function, especially when the function has existing callers.
- ✦ Optional keyword arguments should always be passed by keyword instead of by position.

## Item 20: Use None and Docstrings to Specify Dynamic Default Arguments

Sometimes you need to use a non-static type as a keyword argument's default value. For example, say you want to print logging messages that are marked with the time of the logged event. In the default case, you want the message to include the time when the function was called. You might try the following approach, assuming the default arguments are reevaluated each time the function is called.

```
def log(message, when=datetime.now()):
    print('%s: %s' % (when, message))

log('Hi there!')
sleep(0.1)
log('Hi again!')

>>>
2014-11-15 21:10:10.371432: Hi there!
2014-11-15 21:10:10.371432: Hi again!
```

The timestamps are the same because datetime.now is only executed a single time: when the function is defined. Default argument values are evaluated only once per module load, which usually happens when a program starts up. After the module containing this code is loaded, the datetime.now default argument will never be evaluated again.

The convention for achieving the desired result in Python is to provide a default value of None and to document the actual behavior in the docstring (see Item 49: "Write Docstrings for Every Function, Class, and Module"). When your code sees an argument value of None, you allocate the default value accordingly.

```
def log(message, when=None):
    """Log a message with a timestamp.

    Args:
        message: Message to print.
        when: datetime of when the message occurred.
            Defaults to the present time.
    """
    when = datetime.now() if when is None else when
    print('%s: %s' % (when, message))
```

Now the timestamps will be different.

```
log('Hi there!')
sleep(0.1)
log('Hi again!')

>>>
2014-11-15 21:10:10.472303: Hi there!
2014-11-15 21:10:10.573395: Hi again!
```

Using None for default argument values is especially important when the arguments are mutable. For example, say you want to load a value encoded as JSON data. If decoding the data fails, you want an empty dictionary to be returned by default. You might try this approach.

```
def decode(data, default={}):
    try:
        return json.loads(data)
    except ValueError:
        return default
```

The problem here is the same as the datetime.now example above. The dictionary specified for default will be shared by all calls to decode because default argument values are only evaluated once (at module load time). This can cause extremely surprising behavior.

```
foo = decode('bad data')
foo['stuff'] = 5
bar = decode('also bad')
bar['meep'] = 1
print('Foo:', foo)
print('Bar:', bar)

>>>
Foo: {'stuff': 5, 'meep': 1}
Bar: {'stuff': 5, 'meep': 1}
```

You'd expect two different dictionaries, each with a single key and value. But modifying one seems to also modify the other. The culprit is that `foo` and `bar` are both equal to the `default` parameter. They are the same dictionary object.

```
assert foo is bar
```

The fix is to set the keyword argument default value to `None` and then document the behavior in the function's docstring.

```
def decode(data, default=None):
    """Load JSON data from a string.

    Args:
        data: JSON data to decode.
        default: Value to return if decoding fails.
            Defaults to an empty dictionary.
    """
    if default is None:
        default = {}
    try:
        return json.loads(data)
    except ValueError:
        return default
```

Now, running the same test code as before produces the expected result.

```
foo = decode('bad data')
foo['stuff'] = 5
bar = decode('also bad')
bar['meep'] = 1
print('Foo:', foo)
print('Bar:', bar)

>>>
Foo: {'stuff': 5}
Bar: {'meep': 1}
```

**Things to Remember**

- ✦ Default arguments are only evaluated once: during function definition at module load time. This can cause odd behaviors for dynamic values (like {} or []).
- ✦ Use None as the default value for keyword arguments that have a dynamic value. Document the actual default behavior in the function's docstring.

## Item 21: Enforce Clarity with Keyword-Only Arguments

Passing arguments by keyword is a powerful feature of Python functions (see Item 19: "Provide Optional Behavior with Keyword Arguments"). The flexibility of keyword arguments enables you to write code that will be clear for your use cases.

For example, say you want to divide one number by another but be very careful about special cases. Sometimes you want to ignore ZeroDivisionError exceptions and return infinity instead. Other times, you want to ignore OverflowError exceptions and return zero instead.

```
def safe_division(number, divisor, ignore_overflow,
                  ignore_zero_division):
    try:
        return number / divisor
    except OverflowError:
        if ignore_overflow:
            return 0
        else:
            raise
    except ZeroDivisionError:
        if ignore_zero_division:
            return float('inf')
        else:
            raise
```

Using this function is straightforward. This call will ignore the float overflow from division and will return zero.

```
result = safe_division(1, 10**500, True, False)
print(result)

>>>
0.0
```

This call will ignore the error from dividing by zero and will return infinity.

```
result = safe_division(1, 0, False, True)
print(result)

>>>
inf
```

The problem is that it's easy to confuse the position of the two Boolean arguments that control the exception-ignoring behavior. This can easily cause bugs that are hard to track down. One way to improve the readability of this code is to use keyword arguments. By default, the function can be overly cautious and can always re-raise exceptions.

```
def safe_division_b(number, divisor,
                    ignore_overflow=False,
                    ignore_zero_division=False):
    # ...
```

Then callers can use keyword arguments to specify which of the ignore flags they want to flip for specific operations, overriding the default behavior.

```
safe_division_b(1, 10**500, ignore_overflow=True)
safe_division_b(1, 0, ignore_zero_division=True)
```

The problem is, since these keyword arguments are optional behavior, there's nothing forcing callers of your functions to use keyword arguments for clarity. Even with the new definition of `safe_division_b`, you can still call it the old way with positional arguments.

```
safe_division_b(1, 10**500, True, False)
```

With complex functions like this, it's better to require that callers are clear about their intentions. In Python 3, you can demand clarity by defining your functions with keyword-only arguments. These arguments can only be supplied by keyword, never by position.

Here, I redefine the `safe_division` function to accept keyword-only arguments. The * symbol in the argument list indicates the end of positional arguments and the beginning of keyword-only arguments.

```
def safe_division_c(number, divisor, *,
                    ignore_overflow=False,
                    ignore_zero_division=False):
    # ...
```

Now, calling the function with positional arguments for the keyword arguments won't work.

```
safe_division_c(1, 10**500, True, False)

>>>
TypeError: safe_division_c() takes 2 positional arguments but
➥4 were given
```

Keyword arguments and their default values work as expected.

```
safe_division_c(1, 0, ignore_zero_division=True)  # OK

try:
    safe_division_c(1, 0)
except ZeroDivisionError:
    pass  # Expected
```

### Keyword-Only Arguments in Python 2

Unfortunately, Python 2 doesn't have explicit syntax for specifying keyword-only arguments like Python 3. But you can achieve the same behavior of raising TypeErrors for invalid function calls by using the ** operator in argument lists. The ** operator is similar to the * operator (see Item 18: "Reduce Visual Noise with Variable Positional Arguments"), except that instead of accepting a variable number of positional arguments, it accepts any number of keyword arguments, even when they're not defined.

```
# Python 2
def print_args(*args, **kwargs):
    print 'Positional:', args
    print 'Keyword:   ', kwargs

print_args(1, 2, foo='bar', stuff='meep')

>>>
Positional: (1, 2)
Keyword:    {'foo': 'bar', 'stuff': 'meep'}
```

To make safe_division take keyword-only arguments in Python 2, you have the function accept **kwargs. Then you pop keyword arguments that you expect out of the kwargs dictionary, using the pop method's second argument to specify the default value when the key is missing. Finally, you make sure there are no more keyword arguments left in kwargs to prevent callers from supplying arguments that are invalid.

```
# Python 2
def safe_division_d(number, divisor, **kwargs):
    ignore_overflow = kwargs.pop('ignore_overflow', False)
    ignore_zero_div = kwargs.pop('ignore_zero_division', False)
    if kwargs:
        raise TypeError('Unexpected **kwargs: %r' % kwargs)
    # ...
```

Now, you can call the function with or without keyword arguments.

```
safe_division_d(1, 10)
safe_division_d(1, 0, ignore_zero_division=True)
safe_division_d(1, 10**500, ignore_overflow=True)
```

Trying to pass keyword-only arguments by position won't work, just like in Python 3.

```
safe_division_d(1, 0, False, True)

>>>
TypeError: safe_division_d() takes 2 positional arguments but 4
➥were given
```

Trying to pass unexpected keyword arguments also won't work.

```
safe_division_d(0, 0, unexpected=True)
>>>
TypeError: Unexpected **kwargs: {'unexpected': True}
```

### Things to Remember

- ✦ Keyword arguments make the intention of a function call more clear.
- ✦ Use keyword-only arguments to force callers to supply keyword arguments for potentially confusing functions, especially those that accept multiple Boolean flags.
- ✦ Python 3 supports explicit syntax for keyword-only arguments in functions.
- ✦ Python 2 can emulate keyword-only arguments for functions by using `**kwargs` and manually raising `TypeError` exceptions.

# 3 Classes and Inheritance

As an object-oriented programming language, Python supports a full range of features, such as inheritance, polymorphism, and encapsulation. Getting things done in Python often requires writing new classes and defining how they interact through their interfaces and hierarchies.

Python's classes and inheritance make it easy to express your program's intended behaviors with objects. They allow you to improve and expand functionality over time. They provide flexibility in an environment of changing requirements. Knowing how to use them well enables you to write maintainable code.

## Item 22: Prefer Helper Classes Over Bookkeeping with Dictionaries and Tuples

Python's built-in dictionary type is wonderful for maintaining dynamic internal state over the lifetime of an object. By *dynamic,* I mean situations in which you need to do bookkeeping for an unexpected set of identifiers. For example, say you want to record the grades of a set of students whose names aren't known in advance. You can define a class to store the names in a dictionary instead of using a predefined attribute for each student.

```
class SimpleGradebook(object):
    def __init__(self):
        self._grades = {}

    def add_student(self, name):
        self._grades[name] = []

    def report_grade(self, name, score):
        self._grades[name].append(score)
```

```
    def average_grade(self, name):
        grades = self._grades[name]
        return sum(grades) / len(grades)
```

Using the class is simple.

```
book = SimpleGradebook()
book.add_student('Isaac Newton')
book.report_grade('Isaac Newton', 90)
# ...
print(book.average_grade('Isaac Newton'))

>>>
90.0
```

Dictionaries are so easy to use that there's a danger of overextending them to write brittle code. For example, say you want to extend the SimpleGradebook class to keep a list of grades by subject, not just overall. You can do this by changing the _grades dictionary to map student names (the keys) to yet another dictionary (the values). The innermost dictionary will map subjects (the keys) to grades (the values).

```
class BySubjectGradebook(object):
    def __init__(self):
        self._grades = {}
    def add_student(self, name):
        self._grades[name] = {}
```

This seems straightforward enough. The report_grade and average_grade methods will gain quite a bit of complexity to deal with the multilevel dictionary, but it's manageable.

```
    def report_grade(self, name, subject, grade):
        by_subject = self._grades[name]
        grade_list = by_subject.setdefault(subject, [])
        grade_list.append(grade)

    def average_grade(self, name):
        by_subject = self._grades[name]
        total, count = 0, 0
        for grades in by_subject.values():
            total += sum(grades)
            count += len(grades)
        return total / count
```

Using the class remains simple.

```
book = BySubjectGradebook()
book.add_student('Albert Einstein')
book.report_grade('Albert Einstein', 'Math', 75)
```

```
book.report_grade('Albert Einstein', 'Math', 65)
book.report_grade('Albert Einstein', 'Gym', 90)
book.report_grade('Albert Einstein', 'Gym', 95)
```

Now, imagine your requirements change again. You also want to track the weight of each score toward the overall grade in the class so midterms and finals are more important than pop quizzes. One way to implement this feature is to change the innermost dictionary; instead of mapping subjects (the keys) to grades (the values), I can use the tuple `(score, weight)` as values.

```
class WeightedGradebook(object):
    # ...
    def report_grade(self, name, subject, score, weight):
        by_subject = self._grades[name]
        grade_list = by_subject.setdefault(subject, [])
        grade_list.append((score, weight))
```

Although the changes to `report_grade` seem simple—just make the value a tuple—the `average_grade` method now has a loop within a loop and is difficult to read.

```
    def average_grade(self, name):
        by_subject = self._grades[name]
        score_sum, score_count = 0, 0
        for subject, scores in by_subject.items():
            subject_avg, total_weight = 0, 0
            for score, weight in scores:
                # ...
        return score_sum / score_count
```

Using the class has also gotten more difficult. It's unclear what all of the numbers in the positional arguments mean.

```
book.report_grade('Albert Einstein', 'Math', 80, 0.10)
```

When you see complexity like this happen, it's time to make the leap from dictionaries and tuples to a hierarchy of classes.

At first, you didn't know you'd need to support weighted grades, so the complexity of additional helper classes seemed unwarranted. Python's built-in dictionary and tuple types made it easy to keep going, adding layer after layer to the internal bookkeeping. But you should avoid doing this for more than one level of nesting (i.e., avoid dictionaries that contain dictionaries). It makes your code hard to read by other programmers and sets you up for a maintenance nightmare.

As soon as you realize the bookkeeping is getting complicated, break it all out into classes. This lets you provide well-defined interfaces that better encapsulate your data. This also enables you to create a layer of abstraction between your interfaces and your concrete implementations.

## Refactoring to Classes

You can start moving to classes at the bottom of the dependency tree: a single grade. A class seems too heavyweight for such simple information. A tuple, though, seems appropriate because grades are immutable. Here, I use the tuple (score, weight) to track grades in a list:

```
grades = []
grades.append((95, 0.45))
# ...
total = sum(score * weight for score, weight in grades)
total_weight = sum(weight for _, weight in grades)
average_grade = total / total_weight
```

The problem is that plain tuples are positional. When you want to associate more information with a grade, like a set of notes from the teacher, you'll need to rewrite every usage of the two-tuple to be aware that there are now three items present instead of two. Here, I use _ (the underscore variable name, a Python convention for unused variables) to capture the third entry in the tuple and just ignore it:

```
grades = []
grades.append((95, 0.45, 'Great job'))
# ...
total = sum(score * weight for score, weight, _ in grades)
total_weight = sum(weight for _, weight, _ in grades)
average_grade = total / total_weight
```

This pattern of extending tuples longer and longer is similar to deepening layers of dictionaries. As soon as you find yourself going longer than a two-tuple, it's time to consider another approach.

The namedtuple type in the collections module does exactly what you need. It lets you easily define tiny, immutable data classes.

```
import collections
Grade = collections.namedtuple('Grade', ('score', 'weight'))
```

These classes can be constructed with positional or keyword arguments. The fields are accessible with named attributes. Having named attributes makes it easy to move from a namedtuple to your own class later if your requirements change again and you need to add behaviors to the simple data containers.

### Limitations of namedtuple

Although useful in many circumstances, it's important to understand when namedtuple can cause more harm than good.

- You can't specify default argument values for namedtuple classes. This makes them unwieldy when your data may have many optional properties. If you find yourself using more than a handful of attributes, defining your own class may be a better choice.
- The attribute values of namedtuple instances are still accessible using numerical indexes and iteration. Especially in externalized APIs, this can lead to unintentional usage that makes it harder to move to a real class later. If you're not in control of all of the usage of your namedtuple instances, it's better to define your own class.

Next, you can write a class to represent a single subject that contains a set of grades.

```
class Subject(object):
    def __init__(self):
        self._grades = []

    def report_grade(self, score, weight):
        self._grades.append(Grade(score, weight))

    def average_grade(self):
        total, total_weight = 0, 0
        for grade in self._grades:
            total += grade.score * grade.weight
            total_weight += grade.weight
        return total / total_weight
```

Then you would write a class to represent a set of subjects that are being studied by a single student.

```
class Student(object):
    def __init__(self):
        self._subjects = {}

    def subject(self, name):
        if name not in self._subjects:
            self._subjects[name] = Subject()
        return self._subjects[name]
```

```
    def average_grade(self):
        total, count = 0, 0
        for subject in self._subjects.values():
            total += subject.average_grade()
            count += 1
        return total / count
```

Finally, you'd write a container for all of the students keyed dynamically by their names.

```
class Gradebook(object):
    def __init__(self):
        self._students = {}

    def student(self, name):
        if name not in self._students:
            self._students[name] = Student()
        return self._students[name]
```

The line count of these classes is almost double the previous implementation's size. But this code is much easier to read. The example driving the classes is also more clear and extensible.

```
book = Gradebook()
albert = book.student('Albert Einstein')
math = albert.subject('Math')
math.report_grade(80, 0.10)
# ...
print(albert.average_grade())

>>>
81.5
```

If necessary, you can write backwards-compatible methods to help migrate usage of the old API style to the new hierarchy of objects.

### Things to Remember

- ✦ Avoid making dictionaries with values that are other dictionaries or long tuples.
- ✦ Use `namedtuple` for lightweight, immutable data containers before you need the flexibility of a full class.
- ✦ Move your bookkeeping code to use multiple helper classes when your internal state dictionaries get complicated.

## Item 23: Accept Functions for Simple Interfaces Instead of Classes

Many of Python's built-in APIs allow you to customize behavior by passing in a function. These *hooks* are used by APIs to call back your code while they execute. For example, the `list` type's `sort` method takes an optional `key` argument that's used to determine each index's value for sorting. Here, I sort a list of names based on their lengths by providing a `lambda` expression as the `key` hook:

```
names = ['Socrates', 'Archimedes', 'Plato', 'Aristotle']
names.sort(key=lambda x: len(x))
print(names)

>>>
['Plato', 'Socrates', 'Aristotle', 'Archimedes']
```

In other languages, you might expect hooks to be defined by an abstract class. In Python, many hooks are just stateless functions with well-defined arguments and return values. Functions are ideal for hooks because they are easier to describe and simpler to define than classes. Functions work as hooks because Python has *first-class functions*: Functions and methods can be passed around and referenced like any other value in the language.

For example, say you want to customize the behavior of the `defaultdict` class (see Item 46: "Use Built-in Algorithms and Data Structures" for details). This data structure allows you to supply a function that will be called each time a missing key is accessed. The function must return the default value the missing key should have in the dictionary. Here, I define a hook that logs each time a key is missing and returns `0` for the default value:

```
def log_missing():
    print('Key added')
    return 0
```

Given an initial dictionary and a set of desired increments, I can cause the `log_missing` function to run and print twice (for `'red'` and `'orange'`).

```
current = {'green': 12, 'blue': 3}
increments = [
    ('red', 5),
    ('blue', 17),
    ('orange', 9),
]
```

```
result = defaultdict(log_missing, current)
print('Before:', dict(result))
for key, amount in increments:
    result[key] += amount
print('After: ', dict(result))

>>>
Before: {'green': 12, 'blue': 3}
Key added
Key added
After:  {'orange': 9, 'green': 12, 'blue': 20, 'red': 5}
```

Supplying functions like `log_missing` makes APIs easy to build and test because it separates side effects from deterministic behavior. For example, say you now want the default value hook passed to `defaultdict` to count the total number of keys that were missing. One way to achieve this is using a stateful closure (see Item 15: "Know How Closures Interact with Variable Scope" for details). Here, I define a helper function that uses such a closure as the default value hook:

```
def increment_with_report(current, increments):
    added_count = 0

    def missing():
        nonlocal added_count  # Stateful closure
        added_count += 1
        return 0

    result = defaultdict(missing, current)
    for key, amount in increments:
        result[key] += amount

    return result, added_count
```

Running this function produces the expected result (2), even though the `defaultdict` has no idea that the `missing` hook maintains state. This is another benefit of accepting simple functions for interfaces. It's easy to add functionality later by hiding state in a closure.

```
result, count = increment_with_report(current, increments)
assert count == 2
```

The problem with defining a closure for stateful hooks is that it's harder to read than the stateless function example. Another approach is to define a small class that encapsulates the state you want to track.

```
class CountMissing(object):
    def __init__(self):
        self.added = 0

    def missing(self):
        self.added += 1
        return 0
```

In other languages, you might expect that now defaultdict would have to be modified to accommodate the interface of CountMissing. But in Python, thanks to first-class functions, you can reference the CountMissing.missing method directly on an object and pass it to defaultdict as the default value hook. It's trivial to have a method satisfy a function interface.

```
counter = CountMissing()
result = defaultdict(counter.missing, current)  # Method ref

for key, amount in increments:
    result[key] += amount
assert counter.added == 2
```

Using a helper class like this to provide the behavior of a stateful closure is clearer than the increment_with_report function above. However, in isolation it's still not immediately obvious wh... .he purpose of the CountMissing class is. Who constructs a CountMissing object? Who calls the missing method? Will the class need other public methods to be added in the future? Until you see its usage with defaultdict, the class is a mystery.

To clarify this situation, Python allows classes to define the __call__ special method. __call__ allows an object to be called just like a function. It also causes the callable built-in function to return True for such an instance.

```
class BetterCountMissing(object):
    def __init__(self):
        self.added = 0

    def __call__(self):
        self.added += 1
        return 0

counter = BetterCountMissing()
counter()
assert callable(counter)
```

Here, I use a BetterCountMissing instance as the default value hook for a defaultdict to track the number of missing keys that were added:

```
counter = BetterCountMissing()
result = defaultdict(counter, current)  # Relies on __call__
for key, amount in increments:
    result[key] += amount
assert counter.added == 2
```

This is much clearer than the CountMissing.missing example. The __call__ method indicates that a class's instances will be used somewhere a function argument would also be suitable (like API hooks). It directs new readers of the code to the entry point that's responsible for the class's primary behavior. It provides a strong hint that the goal of the class is to act as a stateful closure.

Best of all, defaultdict still has no view into what's going on when you use __call__. All that defaultdict requires is a function for the default value hook. Python provides many different ways to satisfy a simple function interface depending on what you need to accomplish.

**Things to Remember**

- ✦ Instead of defining and instantiating classes, functions are often all you need for simple interfaces between components in Python.
- ✦ References to functions and methods in Python are first class, meaning they can be used in expressions like any other type.
- ✦ The __call__ special method enables instances of a class to be called like plain Python functions.
- ✦ When you need a function to maintain state, consider defining a class that provides the __call__ method instead of defining a stateful closure (see Item 15: "Know How Closures Interact with Variable Scope").

## Item 24: Use @classmethod Polymorphism to Construct Objects Generically

In Python, not only do the objects support polymorphism, but the classes do as well. What does that mean, and what is it good for?

Polymorphism is a way for multiple classes in a hierarchy to implement their own unique versions of a method. This allows many classes to fulfill the same interface or abstract base class while providing different functionality (see Item 28: "Inherit from collections.abc for Custom Container Types" for an example).

For example, say you're writing a MapReduce implementation and you want a common class to represent the input data. Here, I define such a class with a read method that must be defined by subclasses:

```
class InputData(object):
    def read(self):
        raise NotImplementedError
```

Here, I have a concrete subclass of InputData that reads data from a file on disk:

```
class PathInputData(InputData):
    def __init__(self, path):
        super().__init__()
        self.path = path

    def read(self):
        return open(self.path).read()
```

You could have any number of InputData subclasses like PathInputData and each of them could implement the standard interface for read to return the bytes of data to process. Other InputData subclasses could read from the network, decompress data transparently, etc.

You'd want a similar abstract interface for the MapReduce worker that consumes the input data in a standard way.

```
class Worker(object):
    def __init__(self, input_data):
        self.input_data = input_data
        self.result = None

    def map(self):
        raise NotImplementedError

    def reduce(self, other):
        raise NotImplementedError
```

Here, I define a concrete subclass of Worker to implement the specific MapReduce function I want to apply: a simple newline counter:

```
class LineCountWorker(Worker):
    def map(self):
        data = self.input_data.read()
        self.result = data.count('\n')

    def reduce(self, other):
        self.result += other.result
```

It may look like this implementation is going great, but I've reached the biggest hurdle in all of this. What connects all of these pieces? I have a nice set of classes with reasonable interfaces and abstractions—but that's only useful once the objects are constructed. What's responsible for building the objects and orchestrating the MapReduce?

The simplest approach is to manually build and connect the objects with some helper functions. Here, I list the contents of a directory and construct a `PathInputData` instance for each file it contains:

```
def generate_inputs(data_dir):
    for name in os.listdir(data_dir):
        yield PathInputData(os.path.join(data_dir, name))
```

Next, I create the `LineCountWorker` instances using the `InputData` instances returned by `generate_inputs`.

```
def create_workers(input_list):
    workers = []
    for input_data in input_list:
        workers.append(LineCountWorker(input_data))
    return workers
```

I execute these `Worker` instances by fanning out the `map` step to multiple threads (see Item 37 "Use Threads for Blocking I/O, Avoid for Parallelism"). Then, I call `reduce` repeatedly to combine the results into one final value.

```
def execute(workers):
    threads = [Thread(target=w.map) for w in workers]
    for thread in threads: thread.start()
    for thread in threads: thread.join()

    first, rest = workers[0], workers[1:]
    for worker in rest:
        first.reduce(worker)
    return first.result
```

Finally, I connect all of the pieces together in a function to run each step.

```
def mapreduce(data_dir):
    inputs = generate_inputs(data_dir)
    workers = create_workers(inputs)
    return execute(workers)
```

Running this function on a set of test input files works great.

```
from tempfile import TemporaryDirectory

def write_test_files(tmpdir):
    # ...

with TemporaryDirectory() as tmpdir:
    write_test_files(tmpdir)
    result = mapreduce(tmpdir)

print('There are', result, 'lines')

>>>
There are 4360 lines
```

What's the problem? The huge issue is the mapreduce function is not generic at all. If you want to write another InputData or Worker subclass, you would also have to rewrite the generate_inputs, create_workers, and mapreduce functions to match.

This problem boils down to needing a generic way to construct objects. In other languages, you'd solve this problem with constructor polymorphism, requiring that each InputData subclass provides a special constructor that can be used generically by the helper methods that orchestrate the MapReduce. The trouble is that Python only allows for the single constructor method __init__. It's unreasonable to require every InputData subclass to have a compatible constructor.

The best way to solve this problem is with @classmethod polymorphism. This is exactly like the instance method polymorphism I used for InputData.read, except that it applies to whole classes instead of their constructed objects.

Let me apply this idea to the MapReduce classes. Here, I extend the InputData class with a generic class method that's responsible for creating new InputData instances using a common interface:

```
class GenericInputData(object):
    def read(self):
        raise NotImplementedError

    @classmethod
    def generate_inputs(cls, config):
        raise NotImplementedError
```

I have generate_inputs take a dictionary with a set of configuration parameters that are up to the InputData concrete subclass to interpret. Here, I use the config to find the directory to list for input files:

```
class PathInputData(GenericInputData):
    # ...
    def read(self):
        return open(self.path).read()

    @classmethod
    def generate_inputs(cls, config):
        data_dir = config['data_dir']
        for name in os.listdir(data_dir):
            yield cls(os.path.join(data_dir, name))
```

Similarly, I can make the create_workers helper part of the GenericWorker class. Here, I use the input_class parameter, which must be a subclass of GenericInputData, to generate the necessary inputs. I construct instances of the GenericWorker concrete subclass using cls() as a generic constructor.

```
class GenericWorker(object):
    # ...
    def map(self):
        raise NotImplementedError

    def reduce(self, other):
        raise NotImplementedError

    @classmethod
    def create_workers(cls, input_class, config):
        workers = []
        for input_data in input_class.generate_inputs(config):
            workers.append(cls(input_data))
        return workers
```

Note that the call to input_class.generate_inputs above is the class polymorphism I'm trying to show. You can also see how create_workers calling cls provides an alternate way to construct GenericWorker objects besides using the __init__ method directly.

The effect on my concrete GenericWorker subclass is nothing more than changing its parent class.

```
class LineCountWorker(GenericWorker):
    # ...
```

And finally, I can rewrite the mapreduce function to be completely generic.

```
def mapreduce(worker_class, input_class, config):
    workers = worker_class.create_workers(input_class, config)
    return execute(workers)
```

Running the new worker on a set of test files produces the same result as the old implementation. The difference is that the mapreduce function requires more parameters so that it can operate generically.

```
with TemporaryDirectory() as tmpdir:
    write_test_files(tmpdir)
    config = {'data_dir': tmpdir}
    result = mapreduce(LineCountWorker, PathInputData, config)
```

Now you can write other GenericInputData and GenericWorker classes as you wish and not have to rewrite any of the glue code.

### Things to Remember

- ✦ Python only supports a single constructor per class, the __init__ method.
- ✦ Use @classmethod to define alternative constructors for your classes.
- ✦ Use class method polymorphism to provide generic ways to build and connect concrete subclasses.

## Item 25: Initialize Parent Classes with super

The old way to initialize a parent class from a child class is to directly call the parent class's __init__ method with the child instance.

```
class MyBaseClass(object):
    def __init__(self, value):
        self.value = value

class MyChildClass(MyBaseClass):
    def __init__(self):
        MyBaseClass.__init__(self, 5)
```

This approach works fine for simple hierarchies but breaks down in many cases.

If your class is affected by multiple inheritance (something to avoid in general; see Item 26: "Use Multiple Inheritance Only for Mix-in Utility Classes"), calling the superclasses' __init__ methods directly can lead to unpredictable behavior.

One problem is that the `__init__` call order isn't specified across all subclasses. For example, here I define two parent classes that operate on the instance's `value` field:

```
class TimesTwo(object):
    def __init__(self):
        self.value *= 2

class PlusFive(object):
    def __init__(self):
        self.value += 5
```

This class defines its parent classes in one ordering.

```
class OneWay(MyBaseClass, TimesTwo, PlusFive):
    def __init__(self, value):
        MyBaseClass.__init__(self, value)
        TimesTwo.__init__(self)
        PlusFive.__init__(self)
```

And constructing it produces a result that matches the parent class ordering.

```
foo = OneWay(5)
print('First ordering is (5 * 2) + 5 =', foo.value)

>>>
First ordering is (5 * 2) + 5 = 15
```

Here's another class that defines the same parent classes but in a different ordering:

```
class AnotherWay(MyBaseClass, PlusFive, TimesTwo):
    def __init__(self, value):
        MyBaseClass.__init__(self, value)
        TimesTwo.__init__(self)
        PlusFive.__init__(self)
```

However, I left the calls to the parent class constructors `PlusFive.__init__` and `TimesTwo.__init__` in the same order as before, causing this class's behavior not to match the order of the parent classes in its definition.

```
bar = AnotherWay(5)
print('Second ordering still is', bar.value)

>>>
Second ordering still is 15
```

Another problem occurs with diamond inheritance. Diamond inheritance happens when a subclass inherits from two separate classes that have the same superclass somewhere in the hierarchy. Diamond inheritance causes the common superclass's `__init__` method to run multiple times, causing unexpected behavior. For example, here I define two child classes that inherit from `MyBaseClass`.

```
class TimesFive(MyBaseClass):
    def __init__(self, value):
        MyBaseClass.__init__(self, value)
        self.value *= 5

class PlusTwo(MyBaseClass):
    def __init__(self, value):
        MyBaseClass.__init__(self, value)
        self.value += 2
```

Then, I define a child class that inherits from both of these classes, making `MyBaseClass` the top of the diamond.

```
class ThisWay(TimesFive, PlusTwo):
    def __init__(self, value):
        TimesFive.__init__(self, value)
        PlusTwo.__init__(self, value)

foo = ThisWay(5)
print('Should be (5 * 5) + 2 = 27 but is', foo.value)

>>>
Should be (5 * 5) + 2 = 27 but is 7
```

The output should be 27 because `(5 * 5) + 2 = 27`. But the call to the second parent class's constructor, `PlusTwo.__init__`, causes `self.value` to be reset back to 5 when `MyBaseClass.__init__` gets called a second time.

To solve these problems, Python 2.2 added the `super` built-in function and defined the method resolution order (MRO). The MRO standardizes which superclasses are initialized before others (e.g., depth-first, left-to-right). It also ensures that common superclasses in diamond hierarchies are only run once.

Here, I create a diamond-shaped class hierarchy again, but this time I use `super` (in the Python 2 style) to initialize the parent class:

```
# Python 2
class TimesFiveCorrect(MyBaseClass):
    def __init__(self, value):
        super(TimesFiveCorrect, self).__init__(value)
        self.value *= 5
```

```
class PlusTwoCorrect(MyBaseClass):
    def __init__(self, value):
        super(PlusTwoCorrect, self).__init__(value)
        self.value += 2
```

Now the top part of the diamond, MyBaseClass.__init__, is only run a single time. The other parent classes are run in the order specified in the class statement.

```
# Python 2
class GoodWay(TimesFiveCorrect, PlusTwoCorrect):
    def __init__(self, value):
        super(GoodWay, self).__init__(value)

foo = GoodWay(5)
print 'Should be 5 * (5 + 2) = 35 and is', foo.value

>>>
Should be 5 * (5 + 2) = 35 and is 35
```

This order may seem backwards at first. Shouldn't TimesFiveCorrect.__init__ have run first? Shouldn't the result be (5 * 5) + 2 = 27? The answer is no. This ordering matches what the MRO defines for this class. The MRO ordering is available on a class method called mro.

```
from pprint import pprint
pprint(GoodWay.mro())

>>>
[<class '__main__.GoodWay'>,
<class '__main__.TimesFiveCorrect'>,
<class '__main__.PlusTwoCorrect'>,
<class '__main__.MyBaseClass'>,
<class 'object'>]
```

When I call GoodWay(5), it in turn calls TimesFiveCorrect.__init__, which calls PlusTwoCorrect.__init__, which calls MyBaseClass.__init__. Once this reaches the top of the diamond, then all of the initialization methods actually do their work in the opposite order from how their __init__ functions were called. MyBaseClass.__init__ assigns the value to 5. PlusTwoCorrect.__init__ adds 2 to make value equal 7. TimesFiveCorrect.__init__ multiplies it by 5 to make value equal 35.

The super built-in function works well, but it still has two noticeable problems in Python 2:

- Its syntax is a bit verbose. You have to specify the class you're in, the self object, the method name (usually __init__), and all the arguments. This construction can be confusing to new Python programmers.

- You have to specify the current class by name in the call to super. If you ever change the class's name—a very common activity when improving a class hierarchy—you also need to update every call to super.

Thankfully, Python 3 fixes these issues by making calls to super with no arguments equivalent to calling super with `__class__` and self specified. In Python 3, you should always use super because it's clear, concise, and always does the right thing.

```
class Explicit(MyBaseClass):
    def __init__(self, value):
        super(__class__, self).__init__(value * 2)

class Implicit(MyBaseClass):
    def __init__(self, value):
        super().__init__(value * 2)

assert Explicit(10).value == Implicit(10).value
```

This works because Python 3 lets you reliably reference the current class in methods using the `__class__` variable. This doesn't work in Python 2 because `__class__` isn't defined. You may guess that you could use `self.__class__` as an argument to super, but this breaks because of the way super is implemented in Python 2.

### Things to Remember

- ✦ Python's standard method resolution order (MRO) solves the problems of superclass initialization order and diamond inheritance.
- ✦ Always use the super built-in function to initialize parent classes.

## Item 26: Use Multiple Inheritance Only for Mix-in Utility Classes

Python is an object-oriented language with built-in facilities for making multiple inheritance tractable (see Item 25: "Initialize Parent Classes with super"). However, it's better to avoid multiple inheritance altogether.

If you find yourself desiring the convenience and encapsulation that comes with multiple inheritance, consider writing a *mix-in* instead. A mix-in is a small class that only defines a set of additional methods that a class should provide. Mix-in classes don't define their own instance attributes nor require their `__init__` constructor to be called.

Writing mix-ins is easy because Python makes it trivial to inspect the current state of any object regardless of its type. Dynamic inspection lets you write generic functionality a single time, in a mix-in, that can be applied to many other classes. Mix-ins can be composed and layered to minimize repetitive code and maximize reuse.

For example, say you want the ability to convert a Python object from its in-memory representation to a dictionary that's ready for serialization. Why not write this functionality generically so you can use it with all of your classes?

Here, I define an example mix-in that accomplishes this with a new public method that's added to any class that inherits from it:

```
class ToDictMixin(object):
    def to_dict(self):
        return self._traverse_dict(self.__dict__)
```

The implementation details are straightforward and rely on dynamic attribute access using `hasattr`, dynamic type inspection with `isinstance`, and accessing the instance dictionary `__dict__`.

```
    def _traverse_dict(self, instance_dict):
        output = {}
        for key, value in instance_dict.items():
            output[key] = self._traverse(key, value)
        return output

    def _traverse(self, key, value):
        if isinstance(value, ToDictMixin):
            return value.to_dict()
        elif isinstance(value, dict):
            return self._traverse_dict(value)
        elif isinstance(value, list):
            return [self._traverse(key, i) for i in value]
        elif hasattr(value, '__dict__'):
            return self._traverse_dict(value.__dict__)
        else:
            return value
```

Here, I define an example class that uses the mix-in to make a dictionary representation of a binary tree:

```
class BinaryTree(ToDictMixin):
    def __init__(self, value, left=None, right=None):
```

```
        self.value = value
        self.left = left
        self.right = right
```

Translating a large number of related Python objects into a dictionary becomes easy.

```
tree = BinaryTree(10,
    left=BinaryTree(7, right=BinaryTree(9)),
    right=BinaryTree(13, left=BinaryTree(11)))
print(tree.to_dict())

>>>
{'left': {'left': None,
          'right': {'left': None, 'right': None, 'value': 9},
          'value': 7},
 'right': {'left': {'left': None, 'right': None, 'value': 11},
           'right': None,
           'value': 13},
 'value': 10}
```

The best part about mix-ins is that you can make their generic functionality pluggable so behaviors can be overridden when required. For example, here I define a subclass of BinaryTree that holds a reference to its parent. This circular reference would cause the default implementation of ToDictMixin.to_dict to loop forever.

```
class BinaryTreeWithParent(BinaryTree):
    def __init__(self, value, left=None,
                 right=None, parent=None):
        super().__init__(value, left=left, right=right)
        self.parent = parent
```

The solution is to override the ToDictMixin._traverse method in the BinaryTreeWithParent class to only process values that matter, preventing cycles encountered by the mix-in. Here, I override the _traverse method to not traverse the parent and just insert its numerical value:

```
    def _traverse(self, key, value):
        if (isinstance(value, BinaryTreeWithParent) and
                key == 'parent'):
            return value.value  # Prevent cycles
        else:
            return super()._traverse(key, value)
```

Calling BinaryTreeWithParent.to_dict will work without issue because the circular referencing properties aren't followed.

```
root = BinaryTreeWithParent(10)
root.left = BinaryTreeWithParent(7, parent=root)
root.left.right = BinaryTreeWithParent(9, parent=root.left)
print(root.to_dict())

>>>
{'left': {'left': None,
          'parent': 10,
          'right': {'left': None,
                    'parent': 7,
                    'right': None,
                    'value': 9},
          'value': 7},
 'parent': None,
 'right': None,
 'value': 10}
```

By defining BinaryTreeWithParent._traverse, I've also enabled any class that has an attribute of type BinaryTreeWithParent to automatically work with ToDictMixin.

```
class NamedSubTree(ToDictMixin):
    def __init__(self, name, tree_with_parent):
        self.name = name
        self.tree_with_parent = tree_with_parent

my_tree = NamedSubTree('foobar', root.left.right)
print(my_tree.to_dict())  # No infinite loop

>>>
{'name': 'foobar',
 'tree_with_parent': {'left': None,
                      'parent': 7,
                      'right': None,
                      'value': 9}}
```

Mix-ins can also be composed together. For example, say you want a mix-in that provides generic JSON serialization for any class. You can do this by assuming that a class provides a to_dict method (which may or may not be provided by the ToDictMixin class).

```
class JsonMixin(object):
    @classmethod
    def from_json(cls, data):
        kwargs = json.loads(data)
        return cls(**kwargs)
```

```
    def to_json(self):
        return json.dumps(self.to_dict())
```

Note how the JsonMixin class defines both instance methods and class methods. Mix-ins let you add either kind of behavior. In this example, the only requirements of the JsonMixin are that the class has a to_dict method and its __init__ method takes keyword arguments (see Item 19: "Provide Optional Behavior with Keyword Arguments").

This mix-in makes it simple to create hierarchies of utility classes that can be serialized to and from JSON with little boilerplate. For example, here I have a hierarchy of data classes representing parts of a datacenter topology:

```
class DatacenterRack(ToDictMixin, JsonMixin):
    def __init__(self, switch=None, machines=None):
        self.switch = Switch(**switch)
        self.machines = [
            Machine(**kwargs) for kwargs in machines]


class Switch(ToDictMixin, JsonMixin):
    # ...


class Machine(ToDictMixin, JsonMixin):
    # ...
```

Serializing these classes to and from JSON is simple. Here, I verify that the data is able to be sent round-trip through serializing and deserializing:

```
serialized = """{
    "switch": {"ports": 5, "speed": 1e9},
    "machines": [
        {"cores": 8, "ram": 32e9, "disk": 5e12},
        {"cores": 4, "ram": 16e9, "disk": 1e12},
        {"cores": 2, "ram": 4e9, "disk": 500e9}
    ]
}"""

deserialized = DatacenterRack.from_json(serialized)
roundtrip = deserialized.to_json()
assert json.loads(serialized) == json.loads(roundtrip)
```

When you use mix-ins like this, it's also fine if the class already inherits from JsonMixin higher up in the object hierarchy. The resulting class will behave the same way.

### Things to Remember

- ✦ Avoid using multiple inheritance if mix-in classes can achieve the same outcome.
- ✦ Use pluggable behaviors at the instance level to provide per-class customization when mix-in classes may require it.
- ✦ Compose mix-ins to create complex functionality from simple behaviors.

## Item 27: Prefer Public Attributes Over Private Ones

In Python, there are only two types of attribute visibility for a class's attributes: *public* and *private*.

```
class MyObject(object):
    def __init__(self):
        self.public_field = 5
        self.__private_field = 10

    def get_private_field(self):
        return self.__private_field
```

Public attributes can be accessed by anyone using the dot operator on the object.

```
foo = MyObject()
assert foo.public_field == 5
```

Private fields are specified by prefixing an attribute's name with a double underscore. They can be accessed directly by methods of the containing class.

```
assert foo.get_private_field() == 10
```

Directly accessing private fields from outside the class raises an exception.

```
foo.__private_field

>>>
AttributeError: 'MyObject' object has no attribute
➥'__private_field'
```

Class methods also have access to private attributes because they are declared within the surrounding `class` block.

```
class MyOtherObject(object):
    def __init__(self):
        self.__private_field = 71
```

```
    @classmethod
    def get_private_field_of_instance(cls, instance):
        return instance.__private_field

bar = MyOtherObject()
assert MyOtherObject.get_private_field_of_instance(bar) == 71
```

As you'd expect with private fields, a subclass can't access its parent class's private fields.

```
class MyParentObject(object):
    def __init__(self):
        self.__private_field = 71

class MyChildObject(MyParentObject):
    def get_private_field(self):
        return self.__private_field

baz = MyChildObject()
baz.get_private_field()

>>>
AttributeError: 'MyChildObject' object has no attribute
➥'_MyChildObject__private_field'
```

The private attribute behavior is implemented with a simple transformation of the attribute name. When the Python compiler sees private attribute access in methods like `MyChildObject.get_private_field`, it translates `__private_field` to access `_MyChildObject__private_field` instead. In this example, `__private_field` was only defined in `MyParentObject.__init__`, meaning the private attribute's real name is `_MyParentObject__private_field`. Accessing the parent's private attribute from the child class fails simply because the transformed attribute name doesn't match.

Knowing this scheme, you can easily access the private attributes of any class, from a subclass or externally, without asking for permission.

```
assert baz._MyParentObject__private_field == 71
```

If you look in the object's attribute dictionary, you'll see that private attributes are actually stored with the names as they appear after the transformation.

```
print(baz.__dict__)

>>>
{'_MyParentObject__private_field': 71}
```

Why doesn't the syntax for private attributes actually enforce strict visibility? The simplest answer is one often-quoted motto of Python: "We are all consenting adults here." Python programmers believe that the benefits of being open outweigh the downsides of being closed.

Beyond that, having the ability to hook language features like attribute access (see Item 32: "Use `__getattr__`, `__getattribute__`, and `__setattr__` for Lazy Attributes") enables you to mess around with the internals of objects whenever you wish. If you can do that, what is the value of Python trying to prevent private attribute access otherwise?

To minimize the damage of accessing internals unknowingly, Python programmers follow a naming convention defined in the style guide (see Item 2: "Follow the PEP 8 Style Guide"). Fields prefixed by a single underscore (like `_protected_field`) are *protected*, meaning external users of the class should proceed with caution.

However, many programmers who are new to Python use private fields to indicate an internal API that shouldn't be accessed by subclasses or externally.

```
class MyClass(object):
    def __init__(self, value):
        self.__value = value

    def get_value(self):
        return str(self.__value)

foo = MyClass(5)
assert foo.get_value() == '5'
```

This is the wrong approach. Inevitably someone, including you, will want to subclass your class to add new behavior or to work around deficiencies in existing methods (like above, how `MyClass.get_value` always returns a string). By choosing private attributes, you're only making subclass overrides and extensions cumbersome and brittle. Your potential subclassers will still access the private fields when they absolutely need to do so.

```
class MyIntegerSubclass(MyClass):
    def get_value(self):
        return int(self._MyClass__value)

foo = MyIntegerSubclass(5)
assert foo.get_value() == 5
```

But if the class hierarchy changes beneath you, these classes will break because the private references are no longer valid. Here, the

MyIntegerSubclass class's immediate parent, MyClass, has had another parent class added called MyBaseClass:

```
class MyBaseClass(object):
    def __init__(self, value):
        self.__value = value
    # ...

class MyClass(MyBaseClass):
    # ...

class MyIntegerSubclass(MyClass):
    def get_value(self):
        return int(self._MyClass__value)
```

The __value attribute is now assigned in the MyBaseClass parent class, not the MyClass parent. That causes the private variable reference self._MyClass__value to break in MyIntegerSubclass.

```
foo = MyIntegerSubclass(5)
foo.get_value()

>>>
AttributeError: 'MyIntegerSubclass' object has no attribute
➥'_MyClass__value'
```

In general, it's better to err on the side of allowing subclasses to do more by using protected attributes. Document each protected field and explain which are internal APIs available to subclasses and which should be left alone entirely. This is as much advice to other programmers as it is guidance for your future self on how to extend your own code safely.

```
class MyClass(object):
    def __init__(self, value):
        # This stores the user-supplied value for the object.
        # It should be coercible to a string. Once assigned for
        # the object it should be treated as immutable.
        self._value = value
```

The only time to seriously consider using private attributes is when you're worried about naming conflicts with subclasses. This problem occurs when a child class unwittingly defines an attribute that was already defined by its parent class.

```
class ApiClass(object):
    def __init__(self):
        self._value = 5
```

```
    def get(self):
        return self._value

class Child(ApiClass):
    def __init__(self):
        super().__init__()
        self._value = 'hello'  # Conflicts

a = Child()
print(a.get(), 'and', a._value, 'should be different')

>>>
hello and hello should be different
```

This is primarily a concern with classes that are part of a public API; the subclasses are out of your control, so you can't refactor to fix the problem. Such a conflict is especially possible with attribute names that are very common (like value). To reduce the risk of this happening, you can use a private attribute in the parent class to ensure that there are no attribute names that overlap with child classes.

```
class ApiClass(object):
    def __init__(self):
        self.__value = 5

    def get(self):
        return self.__value

class Child(ApiClass):
    def __init__(self):
        super().__init__()
        self._value = 'hello'  # OK!

a = Child()
print(a.get(), 'and', a._value, 'are different')

>>>
5 and hello are different
```

### Things to Remember

- ✦ Private attributes aren't rigorously enforced by the Python compiler.
- ✦ Plan from the beginning to allow subclasses to do more with your internal APIs and attributes instead of locking them out by default.

- Use documentation of protected fields to guide subclasses instead of trying to force access control with private attributes.
- Only consider using private attributes to avoid naming conflicts with subclasses that are out of your control.

## Item 28: Inherit from collections.abc for Custom Container Types

Much of programming in Python is defining classes that contain data and describing how such objects relate to each other. Every Python class is a container of some kind, encapsulating attributes and functionality together. Python also provides built-in container types for managing data: lists, tuples, sets, and dictionaries.

When you're designing classes for simple use cases like sequences, it's natural that you'd want to subclass Python's built-in `list` type directly. For example, say you want to create your own custom list type that has additional methods for counting the frequency of its members.

```
class FrequencyList(list):
    def __init__(self, members):
        super().__init__(members)

    def frequency(self):
        counts = {}
        for item in self:
            counts.setdefault(item, 0)
            counts[item] += 1
        return counts
```

By subclassing `list`, you get all of `list`'s standard functionality and preserve the semantics familiar to all Python programmers. Your additional methods can add any custom behaviors you need.

```
foo = FrequencyList(['a', 'b', 'a', 'c', 'b', 'a', 'd'])
print('Length is', len(foo))
foo.pop()
print('After pop:', repr(foo))
print('Frequency:', foo.frequency())

>>>
Length is 7
After pop: ['a', 'b', 'a', 'c', 'b', 'a']
Frequency: {'a': 3, 'c': 1, 'b': 2}
```

Now, imagine you want to provide an object that feels like a `list`, allowing indexing, but isn't a `list` subclass. For example, say you want to provide sequence semantics (like `list` or `tuple`) for a binary tree class.

```
class BinaryNode(object):
    def __init__(self, value, left=None, right=None):
        self.value = value
        self.left = left
        self.right = right
```

How do you make this act like a sequence type? Python implements its container behaviors with instance methods that have special names. When you access a sequence item by index:

```
bar = [1, 2, 3]
bar[0]
```

it will be interpreted as:

```
bar.__getitem__(0)
```

To make the `BinaryNode` class act like a sequence, you can provide a custom implementation of `__getitem__` that traverses the object tree depth first.

```
class IndexableNode(BinaryNode):
    def _search(self, count, index):
        # ...
        # Returns (found, count)

    def __getitem__(self, index):
        found, _ = self._search(0, index)
        if not found:
            raise IndexError('Index out of range')
        return found.value
```

You can construct your binary tree as usual.

```
tree = IndexableNode(
    10,
    left=IndexableNode(
        5,
        left=IndexableNode(2),
        right=IndexableNode(
            6, right=IndexableNode(7))),
    right=IndexableNode(
        15, left=IndexableNode(11)))
```

But you can also access it like a list in addition to tree traversal.

```
print('LRR =', tree.left.right.right.value)
print('Index 0 =', tree[0])
print('Index 1 =', tree[1])
print('11 in the tree?', 11 in tree)
print('17 in the tree?', 17 in tree)
print('Tree is', list(tree))

>>>
LRR = 7
Index 0 = 2
Index 1 = 5
11 in the tree? True
17 in the tree? False
Tree is [2, 5, 6, 7, 10, 11, 15]
```

The problem is that implementing __getitem__ isn't enough to provide all of the sequence semantics you'd expect.

```
len(tree)

>>>
TypeError: object of type 'IndexableNode' has no len()
```

The len built-in function requires another special method named __len__ that must have an implementation for your custom sequence type.

```
class SequenceNode(IndexableNode):
    def __len__(self):
        _, count = self._search(0, None)
        return count

tree = SequenceNode(
    # ...
)

print('Tree has %d nodes' % len(tree))

>>>
Tree has 7 nodes
```

Unfortunately, this still isn't enough. Also missing are the count and index methods that a Python programmer would expect to see on a sequence like list or tuple. Defining your own container types is much harder than it looks.

To avoid this difficulty throughout the Python universe, the built-in collections.abc module defines a set of abstract base classes that provide all of the typical methods for each container type. When you subclass from these abstract base classes and forget to implement required methods, the module will tell you something is wrong.

```
from collections.abc import Sequence

class BadType(Sequence):
    pass

foo = BadType()

>>>
TypeError: Can't instantiate abstract class BadType with
➥abstract methods __getitem__, __len__
```

When you do implement all of the methods required by an abstract base class, as I did above with `SequenceNode`, it will provide all of the additional methods like `index` and `count` for free.

```
class BetterNode(SequenceNode, Sequence):
    pass

tree = BetterNode(
    # ...
)

print('Index of 7 is', tree.index(7))
print('Count of 10 is', tree.count(10))

>>>
Index of 7 is 3
Count of 10 is 1
```

The benefit of using these abstract base classes is even greater for more complex types like `Set` and `MutableMapping`, which have a large number of special methods that need to be implemented to match Python conventions.

### Things to Remember

- Inherit directly from Python's container types (like `list` or `dict`) for simple use cases.
- Beware of the large number of methods required to implement custom container types correctly.
- Have your custom container types inherit from the interfaces defined in `collections.abc` to ensure that your classes match required interfaces and behaviors.

# 4

# Metaclasses and Attributes

Metaclasses are often mentioned in lists of Python's features, but few understand what they accomplish in practice. The name *metaclass* vaguely implies a concept above and beyond a class. Simply put, metaclasses let you intercept Python's `class` statement and provide special behavior each time a class is defined.

Similarly mysterious and powerful are Python's built-in features for dynamically customizing attribute accesses. Along with Python's object-oriented constructs, these facilities provide wonderful tools to ease the transition from simple classes to complex ones.

However, with these powers come many pitfalls. Dynamic attributes enable you to override objects and cause unexpected side effects. Metaclasses can create extremely bizarre behaviors that are unapproachable to newcomers. It's important that you follow the *rule of least surprise* and only use these mechanisms to implement well-understood idioms.

## Item 29: Use Plain Attributes Instead of Get and Set Methods

Programmers coming to Python from other languages may naturally try to implement explicit getter and setter methods in their classes.

```
class OldResistor(object):
    def __init__(self, ohms):
        self._ohms = ohms

    def get_ohms(self):
        return self._ohms

    def set_ohms(self, ohms):
        self._ohms = ohms
```

Using these setters and getters is simple, but it's not Pythonic.

```
r0 = OldResistor(50e3)
print('Before: %5r' % r0.get_ohms())
r0.set_ohms(10e3)
print('After:  %5r' % r0.get_ohms())

>>>
Before: 50000.0
After:  10000.0
```

Such methods are especially clumsy for operations like incrementing in place.

```
r0.set_ohms(r0.get_ohms() + 5e3)
```

These utility methods do help define the interface for your class, making it easier to encapsulate functionality, validate usage, and define boundaries. Those are important goals when designing a class to ensure you don't break callers as your class evolves over time.

In Python, however, you almost never need to implement explicit setter or getter methods. Instead, you should always start your implementations with simple public attributes.

```
class Resistor(object):
    def __init__(self, ohms):
        self.ohms = ohms
        self.voltage = 0
        self.current = 0

r1 = Resistor(50e3)
r1.ohms = 10e3
```

These make operations like incrementing in place natural and clear.

```
r1.ohms += 5e3
```

Later, if you decide you need special behavior when an attribute is set, you can migrate to the `@property` decorator and its corresponding `setter` attribute. Here, I define a new subclass of `Resistor` that lets me vary the `current` by assigning the `voltage` property. Note that in order to work properly the name of both the setter and getter methods must match the intended property name.

```
class VoltageResistance(Resistor):
    def __init__(self, ohms):
        super().__init__(ohms)
        self._voltage = 0
```

```
    @property
    def voltage(self):
        return self._voltage

    @voltage.setter
    def voltage(self, voltage):
        self._voltage = voltage
        self.current = self._voltage / self.ohms
```

Now, assigning the `voltage` property will run the `voltage` setter method, updating the `current` property of the object to match.

```
r2 = VoltageResistance(1e3)
print('Before: %5r amps' % r2.current)
r2.voltage = 10
print('After:  %5r amps' % r2.current)

>>>
Before:     0 amps
After:   0.01 amps
```

Specifying a `setter` on a property also lets you perform type checking and validation on values passed to your class. Here, I define a class that ensures all resistance values are above zero ohms:

```
class BoundedResistance(Resistor):
    def __init__(self, ohms):
        super().__init__(ohms)

    @property
    def ohms(self):
        return self._ohms

    @ohms.setter
    def ohms(self, ohms):
        if ohms <= 0:
            raise ValueError('%f ohms must be > 0' % ohms)
        self._ohms = ohms
```

Assigning an invalid resistance to the attribute raises an exception.

```
r3 = BoundedResistance(1e3)
r3.ohms = 0

>>>
ValueError: 0.000000 ohms must be > 0
```

An exception will also be raised if you pass an invalid value to the constructor.

```
BoundedResistance(-5)
>>>
ValueError: -5.000000 ohms must be > 0
```

This happens because `BoundedResistance.__init__` calls `Resistor.__init__`, which assigns `self.ohms = -5`. That assignment causes the `@ohms.setter` method from `BoundedResistance` to be called, immediately running the validation code before object construction has completed.

You can even use `@property` to make attributes from parent classes immutable.

```
class FixedResistance(Resistor):
    # ...
    @property
    def ohms(self):
        return self._ohms

    @ohms.setter
    def ohms(self, ohms):
        if hasattr(self, '_ohms'):
            raise AttributeError("Can't set attribute")
        self._ohms = ohms
```

Trying to assign to the property after construction raises an exception.

```
r4 = FixedResistance(1e3)
r4.ohms = 2e3

>>>
AttributeError: Can't set attribute
```

The biggest shortcoming of `@property` is that the methods for an attribute can only be shared by subclasses. Unrelated classes can't share the same implementation. However, Python also supports *descriptors* (see Item 31: "Use Descriptors for Reusable `@property` Methods") that enable reusable property logic and many other use cases.

Finally, when you use `@property` methods to implement setters and getters, be sure that the behavior you implement is not surprising. For example, don't set other attributes in getter property methods.

```
class MysteriousResistor(Resistor):
    @property
    def ohms(self):
        self.voltage = self._ohms * self.current
        return self._ohms
    # ...
```

This leads to extremely bizarre behavior.

```
r7 = MysteriousResistor(10)
r7.current = 0.01
print('Before: %5r' % r7.voltage)
r7.ohms
print('After:  %5r' % r7.voltage)

>>>
Before:     0
After:    0.1
```

The best policy is to only modify related object state in `@property.setter` methods. Be sure to avoid any other side effects the caller may not expect beyond the object, such as importing modules dynamically, running slow helper functions, or making expensive database queries. Users of your class will expect its attributes to be like any other Python object: quick and easy. Use normal methods to do anything more complex or slow.

### Things to Remember

- ✦ Define new class interfaces using simple public attributes, and avoid set and get methods.
- ✦ Use `@property` to define special behavior when attributes are accessed on your objects, if necessary.
- ✦ Follow the rule of least surprise and avoid weird side effects in your `@property` methods.
- ✦ Ensure that `@property` methods are fast; do slow or complex work using normal methods.

## Item 30: Consider `@property` Instead of Refactoring Attributes

The built-in `@property` decorator makes it easy for simple accesses of an instance's attributes to act smarter (see Item 29: "Use Plain Attributes Instead of Get and Set Methods"). One advanced but common use of `@property` is transitioning what was once a simple numerical attribute into an on-the-fly calculation. This is extremely helpful because it lets you migrate all existing usage of a class to have new behaviors without rewriting any of the call sites. It also provides an important stopgap for improving your interfaces over time.

For example, say you want to implement a leaky bucket quota using plain Python objects. Here, the Bucket class represents how much quota remains and the duration for which the quota will be available:

```
class Bucket(object):
    def __init__(self, period):
        self.period_delta = timedelta(seconds=period)
        self.reset_time = datetime.now()
        self.quota = 0

    def __repr__(self):
        return 'Bucket(quota=%d)' % self.quota
```

The leaky bucket algorithm works by ensuring that, whenever the bucket is filled, the amount of quota does not carry over from one period to the next.

```
def fill(bucket, amount):
    now = datetime.now()
    if now - bucket.reset_time > bucket.period_delta:
        bucket.quota = 0
        bucket.reset_time = now
    bucket.quota += amount
```

Each time a quota consumer wants to do something, it first must ensure that it can deduct the amount of quota it needs to use.

```
def deduct(bucket, amount):
    now = datetime.now()
    if now - bucket.reset_time > bucket.period_delta:
        return False
    if bucket.quota - amount < 0:
        return False
    bucket.quota -= amount
    return True
```

To use this class, first I fill the bucket.

```
bucket = Bucket(60)
fill(bucket, 100)
print(bucket)

>>>
Bucket(quota=100)
```

Then, I deduct the quota that I need.

```
if deduct(bucket, 99):
    print('Had 99 quota')
else:
    print('Not enough for 99 quota')
print(bucket)

>>>
Had 99 quota
Bucket(quota=1)
```

Eventually, I'm prevented from making progress because I try to deduct more quota than is available. In this case, the bucket's quota level remains unchanged.

```
if deduct(bucket, 3):
    print('Had 3 quota')
else:
    print('Not enough for 3 quota')
print(bucket)

>>>
Not enough for 3 quota
Bucket(quota=1)
```

The problem with this implementation is that I never know what quota level the bucket started with. The quota is deducted over the course of the period until it reaches zero. At that point, `deduct` will always return `False`. When that happens, it would be useful to know whether callers to `deduct` are being blocked because the `Bucket` ran out of quota or because the `Bucket` never had quota in the first place.

To fix this, I can change the class to keep track of the `max_quota` issued in the period and the `quota_consumed` in the period.

```
class Bucket(object):
    def __init__(self, period):
        self.period_delta = timedelta(seconds=period)
        self.reset_time = datetime.now()
        self.max_quota = 0
        self.quota_consumed = 0

    def __repr__(self):
        return ('Bucket(max_quota=%d, quota_consumed=%d)' %
                (self.max_quota, self.quota_consumed))
```

I use a `@property` method to compute the current level of quota on-the-fly using these new attributes.

```
    @property
    def quota(self):
        return self.max_quota - self.quota_consumed
```

When the quota attribute is assigned, I take special action matching the current interface of the class used by `fill` and deduct.

```
    @quota.setter
    def quota(self, amount):
        delta = self.max_quota - amount
        if amount == 0:
            # Quota being reset for a new period
            self.quota_consumed = 0
            self.max_quota = 0
        elif delta < 0:
            # Quota being filled for the new period
            assert self.quota_consumed == 0
            self.max_quota = amount
        else:
            # Quota being consumed during the period
            assert self.max_quota >= self.quota_consumed
            self.quota_consumed += delta
```

Rerunning the demo code from above produces the same results.

```
bucket = Bucket(60)
print('Initial', bucket)
fill(bucket, 100)
print('Filled', bucket)

if deduct(bucket, 99):
    print('Had 99 quota')
else:
    print('Not enough for 99 quota')

print('Now', bucket)

if deduct(bucket, 3):
    print('Had 3 quota')
else:
    print('Not enough for 3 quota')

print('Still', bucket)

>>>
Initial Bucket(max_quota=0, quota_consumed=0)
Filled Bucket(max_quota=100, quota_consumed=0)
```

```
Had 99 quota
Now Bucket(max_quota=100, quota_consumed=99)
Not enough for 3 quota
Still Bucket(max_quota=100, quota_consumed=99)
```

The best part is that the code using Bucket.quota doesn't have to change or know that the class has changed. New usage of Bucket can do the right thing and access max_quota and quota_consumed directly.

I especially like @property because it lets you make incremental progress toward a better data model over time. Reading the Bucket example above, you may have thought to yourself, "fill and deduct should have been implemented as instance methods in the first place." Although you're probably right (see Item 22: "Prefer Helper Classes Over Bookkeeping with Dictionaries and Tuples"), in practice there are many situations in which objects start with poorly defined interfaces or act as dumb data containers. This happens when code grows over time, scope increases, multiple authors contribute without anyone considering long-term hygiene, etc.

@property is a tool to help you address problems you'll come across in real-world code. Don't overuse it. When you find yourself repeatedly extending @property methods, it's probably time to refactor your class instead of further paving over your code's poor design.

### Things to Remember

- ✦ Use @property to give existing instance attributes new functionality.
- ✦ Make incremental progress toward better data models by using @property.
- ✦ Consider refactoring a class and all call sites when you find yourself using @property too heavily.

## Item 31: Use Descriptors for Reusable @property Methods

The big problem with the @property built-in (see Item 29: "Use Plain Attributes Instead of Get and Set Methods" and Item 30: "Consider @property Instead of Refactoring Attributes") is reuse. The methods it decorates can't be reused for multiple attributes of the same class. They also can't be reused by unrelated classes.

For example, say you want a class to validate that the grade received by a student on a homework assignment is a percentage.

```
class Homework(object):
    def __init__(self):
        self._grade = 0

    @property
    def grade(self):
        return self._grade

    @grade.setter
    def grade(self, value):
        if not (0 <= value <= 100):
            raise ValueError('Grade must be between 0 and 100')
        self._grade = value
```

Using an `@property` makes this class easy to use.

```
galileo = Homework()
galileo.grade = 95
```

Say you also want to give the student a grade for an exam, where the exam has multiple subjects, each with a separate grade.

```
class Exam(object):
    def __init__(self):
        self._writing_grade = 0
        self._math_grade = 0

    @staticmethod
    def _check_grade(value):
        if not (0 <= value <= 100):
            raise ValueError('Grade must be between 0 and 100')
```

This quickly gets tedious. Each section of the exam requires adding a new `@property` and related validation.

```
    @property
    def writing_grade(self):
        return self._writing_grade

    @writing_grade.setter
    def writing_grade(self, value):
        self._check_grade(value)
        self._writing_grade = value

    @property
    def math_grade(self):
        return self._math_grade
```

```
    @math_grade.setter
    def math_grade(self, value):
        self._check_grade(value)
        self._math_grade = value
```

Also, this approach is not general. If you want to reuse this percentage validation beyond homework and exams, you'd need to write the @property boilerplate and _check_grade repeatedly.

The better way to do this in Python is to use a *descriptor*. The descriptor protocol defines how attribute access is interpreted by the language. A descriptor class can provide __get__ and __set__ methods that let you reuse the grade validation behavior without any boilerplate. For this purpose, descriptors are also better than mix-ins (see Item 26: "Use Multiple Inheritance Only for Mix-in Utility Classes") because they let you reuse the same logic for many different attributes in a single class.

Here, I define a new class called Exam with class attributes that are Grade instances. The Grade class implements the descriptor protocol. Before I explain how the Grade class works, it's important to understand what Python will do when your code accesses such descriptor attributes on an Exam instance.

```
class Grade(object):
    def __get__(*args, **kwargs):
        # ...

    def __set__(*args, **kwargs):
        # ...

class Exam(object):
    # Class attributes
    math_grade = Grade()
    writing_grade = Grade()
    science_grade = Grade()
```

When you assign a property:

```
exam = Exam()
exam.writing_grade = 40
```

it will be interpreted as:

```
Exam.__dict__['writing_grade'].__set__(exam, 40)
```

When you retrieve a property:

```
print(exam.writing_grade)
```

it will be interpreted as:

```
print(Exam.__dict__['writing_grade'].__get__(exam, Exam))
```

What drives this behavior is the `__getattribute__` method of `object` (see Item 32: "Use `__getattr__`, `__getattribute__`, and `__setattr__` for Lazy Attributes"). In short, when an `Exam` instance doesn't have an attribute named `writing_grade`, Python will fall back to the `Exam` class's attribute instead. If this class attribute is an object that has `__get__` and `__set__` methods, Python will assume you want to follow the descriptor protocol.

Knowing this behavior and how I used `@property` for grade validation in the `Homework` class, here's a reasonable first attempt at implementing the `Grade` descriptor.

```
class Grade(object):
    def __init__(self):
        self._value = 0

    def __get__(self, instance, instance_type):
        return self._value

    def __set__(self, instance, value):
        if not (0 <= value <= 100):
            raise ValueError('Grade must be between 0 and 100')
        self._value = value
```

Unfortunately, this is wrong and will result in broken behavior. Accessing multiple attributes on a single `Exam` instance works as expected.

```
first_exam = Exam()
first_exam.writing_grade = 82
first_exam.science_grade = 99
print('Writing', first_exam.writing_grade)
print('Science', first_exam.science_grade)

>>>
Writing 82
Science 99
```

But accessing these attributes on multiple `Exam` instances will have unexpected behavior.

```
second_exam = Exam()
second_exam.writing_grade = 75
print('Second', second_exam.writing_grade, 'is right')
print('First ', first_exam.writing_grade, 'is wrong')

>>>
Second 75 is right
First  75 is wrong
```

The problem is that a single Grade instance is shared across all Exam instances for the class attribute writing_grade. The Grade instance for this attribute is constructed once in the program lifetime when the Exam class is first defined, not each time an Exam instance is created.

To solve this, I need the Grade class to keep track of its value for each unique Exam instance. I can do this by saving the per-instance state in a dictionary.

```
class Grade(object):
    def __init__(self):
        self._values = {}

    def __get__(self, instance, instance_type):
        if instance is None: return self
        return self._values.get(instance, 0)

    def __set__(self, instance, value):
        if not (0 <= value <= 100):
            raise ValueError('Grade must be between 0 and 100')
        self._values[instance] = value
```

This implementation is simple and works well, but there's still one gotcha: It leaks memory. The _values dictionary will hold a reference to every instance of Exam ever passed to __set__ over the lifetime of the program. This causes instances to never have their reference count go to zero, preventing cleanup by the garbage collector.

To fix this, I can use Python's weakref built-in module. This module provides a special class called WeakKeyDictionary that can take the place of the simple dictionary used for _values. The unique behavior of WeakKeyDictionary is that it will remove Exam instances from its set of keys when the runtime knows it's holding the instance's last remaining reference in the program. Python will do the bookkeeping for you and ensure that the _values dictionary will be empty when all Exam instances are no longer in use.

```
class Grade(object):
    def __init__(self):
        self._values = WeakKeyDictionary()
    # ...
```

Using this implementation of the Grade descriptor, everything works as expected.

```
class Exam(object):
    math_grade = Grade()
    writing_grade = Grade()
    science_grade = Grade()
```

```
first_exam = Exam()
first_exam.writing_grade = 82
second_exam = Exam()
second_exam.writing_grade = 75
print('First ', first_exam.writing_grade, 'is right')
print('Second', second_exam.writing_grade, 'is right')

>>>
First  82 is right
Second 75 is right
```

### Things to Remember

- ✦ Reuse the behavior and validation of `@property` methods by defining your own descriptor classes.
- ✦ Use `WeakKeyDictionary` to ensure that your descriptor classes don't cause memory leaks.
- ✦ Don't get bogged down trying to understand exactly how `__getattribute__` uses the descriptor protocol for getting and setting attributes.

## Item 32: Use `__getattr__`, `__getattribute__`, and `__setattr__` for Lazy Attributes

Python's language hooks make it easy to write generic code for gluing systems together. For example, say you want to represent the rows of your database as Python objects. Your database has its schema set. Your code that uses objects corresponding to those rows must also know what your database looks like. However, in Python, the code that connects your Python objects to the database doesn't need to know the schema of your rows; it can be generic.

How is that possible? Plain instance attributes, `@property` methods, and descriptors can't do this because they all need to be defined in advance. Python makes this dynamic behavior possible with the `__getattr__` special method. If your class defines `__getattr__`, that method is called every time an attribute can't be found in an object's instance dictionary.

```
class LazyDB(object):
    def __init__(self):
        self.exists = 5

    def __getattr__(self, name):
        value = 'Value for %s' % name
```

```
        setattr(self, name, value)
        return value
```

Here, I access the missing property foo. This causes Python to call the __getattr__ method above, which mutates the instance dictionary __dict__:

```
data = LazyDB()
print('Before:', data.__dict__)
print('foo:   ', data.foo)
print('After: ', data.__dict__)

>>>
Before: {'exists': 5}
foo:    Value for foo
After:  {'exists': 5, 'foo': 'Value for foo'}
```

Here, I add logging to LazyDB to show when __getattr__ is actually called. Note that I use super().__getattr__() to get the real property value in order to avoid infinite recursion.

```
class LoggingLazyDB(LazyDB):
    def __getattr__(self, name):
        print('Called __getattr__(%s)' % name)
        return super().__getattr__(name)

data = LoggingLazyDB()
print('exists:', data.exists)
print('foo:   ', data.foo)
print('foo:   ', data.foo)

>>>
exists: 5
Called __getattr__(foo)
foo:    Value for foo
foo:    Value for foo
```

The exists attribute is present in the instance dictionary, so __getattr__ is never called for it. The foo attribute is not in the instance dictionary initially, so __getattr__ is called the first time. But the call to __getattr__ for foo also does a setattr, which populates foo in the instance dictionary. This is why the second time I access foo there isn't a call to __getattr__.

This behavior is especially helpful for use cases like lazily accessing schemaless data. __getattr__ runs once to do the hard work of loading a property; all subsequent accesses retrieve the existing result.

Say you also want transactions in this database system. The next time the user accesses a property, you want to know whether the corresponding row in the database is still valid and whether the transaction is still open. The `__getattr__` hook won't let you do this reliably because it will use the object's instance dictionary as the fast path for existing attributes.

To enable this use case, Python has another language hook called `__getattribute__`. This special method is called every time an attribute is accessed on an object, even in cases where it *does* exist in the attribute dictionary. This enables you to do things like check global transaction state on every property access. Here, I define `ValidatingDB` to log each time `__getattribute__` is called:

```
class ValidatingDB(object):
    def __init__(self):
        self.exists = 5

    def __getattribute__(self, name):
        print('Called __getattribute__(%s)' % name)
        try:
            return super().__getattribute__(name)
        except AttributeError:
            value = 'Value for %s' % name
            setattr(self, name, value)
            return value

data = ValidatingDB()
print('exists:', data.exists)
print('foo:   ', data.foo)
print('foo:   ', data.foo)

>>>
Called __getattribute__(exists)
exists: 5
Called __getattribute__(foo)
foo:    Value for foo
Called __getattribute__(foo)
foo:    Value for foo
```

In the event that a dynamically accessed property shouldn't exist, you can raise an `AttributeError` to cause Python's standard missing property behavior for both `__getattr__` and `__getattribute__`.

```
class MissingPropertyDB(object):
    def __getattr__(self, name):
        if name == 'bad_name':
```

```
            raise AttributeError('%s is missing' % name)
        # ...

data = MissingPropertyDB()
data.bad_name

>>>
AttributeError: bad_name is missing
```

Python code implementing generic functionality often relies on the `hasattr` built-in function to determine when properties exist, and the `getattr` built-in function to retrieve property values. These functions also look in the instance dictionary for an attribute name before calling `__getattr__`.

```
data = LoggingLazyDB()
print('Before:      ', data.__dict__)
print('foo exists: ', hasattr(data, 'foo'))
print('After:       ', data.__dict__)
print('foo exists: ', hasattr(data, 'foo'))

>>>
Before:       {'exists': 5}
Called __getattr__(foo)
foo exists:  True
After:        {'exists': 5, 'foo': 'Value for foo'}
foo exists:  True
```

In the example above, `__getattr__` is only called once. In contrast, classes that implement `__getattribute__` will have that method called each time `hasattr` or `getattr` is run on an object.

```
data = ValidatingDB()
print('foo exists: ', hasattr(data, 'foo'))
print('foo exists: ', hasattr(data, 'foo'))

>>>
Called __getattribute__(foo)
foo exists:  True
Called __getattribute__(foo)
foo exists:  True
```

Now, say you want to lazily push data back to the database when values are assigned to your Python object. You can do this with `__setattr__`, a similar language hook that lets you intercept arbitrary attribute assignments. Unlike retrieving an attribute with `__getattr__` and `__getattribute__`, there's no need for two separate methods. The `__setattr__` method is always called every time an attribute is assigned on an instance (either directly or through the setattr built-in function).

```
class SavingDB(object):
    def __setattr__(self, name, value):
        # Save some data to the DB log
        # ...
        super().__setattr__(name, value)
```

Here, I define a logging subclass of SavingDB. Its __setattr__ method is always called on each attribute assignment:

```
class LoggingSavingDB(SavingDB):
    def __setattr__(self, name, value):
        print('Called __setattr__(%s, %r)' % (name, value))
        super().__setattr__(name, value)

data = LoggingSavingDB()
print('Before: ', data.__dict__)
data.foo = 5
print('After:  ', data.__dict__)
data.foo = 7
print('Finally:', data.__dict__)

>>>
Before:  {}
Called __setattr__(foo, 5)
After:   {'foo': 5}
Called __setattr__(foo, 7)
Finally: {'foo': 7}
```

The problem with __getattribute__ and __setattr__ is that they're called on every attribute access for an object, even when you may not want that to happen. For example, say you want attribute accesses on your object to actually look up keys in an associated dictionary.

```
class BrokenDictionaryDB(object):
    def __init__(self, data):
        self._data = {}

    def __getattribute__(self, name):
        print('Called __getattribute__(%s)' % name)
        return self._data[name]
```

This requires accessing self._data from the __getattribute__ method. However, if you actually try to do that, Python will recurse until it reaches its stack limit, and then it'll die.

```
data = BrokenDictionaryDB({'foo': 3})
data.foo

>>>
Called __getattribute__(foo)
Called __getattribute__(_data)
Called __getattribute__(_data)
...
Traceback ...
RuntimeError: maximum recursion depth exceeded
```

The problem is that `__getattribute__` accesses `self._data`, which causes `__getattribute__` to run again, which accesses `self._data` again, and so on. The solution is to use the `super().__getattribute__` method on your instance to fetch values from the instance attribute dictionary. This avoids the recursion.

```
class DictionaryDB(object):
    def __init__(self, data):
        self._data = data

    def __getattribute__(self, name):
        data_dict = super().__getattribute__('_data')
        return data_dict[name]
```

Similarly, you'll need `__setattr__` methods that modify attributes on an object to use `super().__setattr__`.

### Things to Remember

- ✦ Use `__getattr__` and `__setattr__` to lazily load and save attributes for an object.
- ✦ Understand that `__getattr__` only gets called once when accessing a missing attribute, whereas `__getattribute__` gets called every time an attribute is accessed.
- ✦ Avoid infinite recursion in `__getattribute__` and `__setattr__` by using methods from `super()` (i.e., the `object` class) to access instance attributes directly.

## Item 33: Validate Subclasses with Metaclasses

One of the simplest applications of metaclasses is verifying that a class was defined correctly. When you're building a complex class hierarchy, you may want to enforce style, require overriding methods, or have strict relationships between class attributes. Metaclasses enable these use cases by providing a reliable way to run your validation code each time a new subclass is defined.

Often a class's validation code runs in the `__init__` method, when an object of the class's type is constructed (see Item 28: "Inherit from `collections.abc` for Custom Container Types" for an example). Using metaclasses for validation can raise errors much earlier.

Before I get into how to define a metaclass for validating subclasses, it's important to understand the metaclass action for standard objects. A metaclass is defined by inheriting from `type`. In the default case, a metaclass receives the contents of associated `class` statements in its `__new__` method. Here, you can modify the class information before the type is actually constructed:

```
class Meta(type):
    def __new__(meta, name, bases, class_dict):
        print((meta, name, bases, class_dict))
        return type.__new__(meta, name, bases, class_dict)

class MyClass(object, metaclass=Meta):
    stuff = 123

    def foo(self):
        pass
```

The metaclass has access to the name of the class, the parent classes it inherits from, and all of the class attributes that were defined in the class's body.

```
>>>
(<class '__main__.Meta'>,
 'MyClass',
 (<class 'object'>,),
 {'__module__': '__main__',
  '__qualname__': 'MyClass',
  'foo': <function MyClass.foo at 0x102c7dd08>,
  'stuff': 123})
```

Python 2 has slightly different syntax and specifies a metaclass using the `__metaclass__` class attribute. The `Meta.__new__` interface is the same.

```
# Python 2
class Meta(type):
    def __new__(meta, name, bases, class_dict):
        # ...
```

```
class MyClassInPython2(object):
    __metaclass__ = Meta
    # ...
```

You can add functionality to the `Meta.__new__` method in order to validate all of the parameters of a class before it's defined. For example, say you want to represent any type of multisided polygon. You can do this by defining a special validating metaclass and using it in the base class of your polygon class hierarchy. Note that it's important not to apply the same validation to the base class.

```
class ValidatePolygon(type):
    def __new__(meta, name, bases, class_dict):
        # Don't validate the abstract Polygon class
        if bases != (object,):
            if class_dict['sides'] < 3:
                raise ValueError('Polygons need 3+ sides')
        return type.__new__(meta, name, bases, class_dict)

class Polygon(object, metaclass=ValidatePolygon):
    sides = None  # Specified by subclasses

    @classmethod
    def interior_angles(cls):
        return (cls.sides - 2) * 180

class Triangle(Polygon):
    sides = 3
```

If you try to define a polygon with fewer than three sides, the validation will cause the `class` statement to fail immediately after the `class` statement body. This means your program will not even be able to start running when you define such a class.

```
print('Before class')
class Line(Polygon):
    print('Before sides')
    sides = 1
    print('After sides')
print('After class')

>>>
Before class
Before sides
After sides
Traceback ...
ValueError: Polygons need 3+ sides
```

### Things to Remember

- ✦ Use metaclasses to ensure that subclasses are well formed at the time they are defined, before objects of their type are constructed.
- ✦ Metaclasses have slightly different syntax in Python 2 vs. Python 3.
- ✦ The `__new__` method of metaclasses is run after the class statement's entire body has been processed.

## Item 34: Register Class Existence with Metaclasses

Another common use of metaclasses is to automatically register types in your program. Registration is useful for doing reverse lookups, where you need to map a simple identifier back to a corresponding class.

For example, say you want to implement your own serialized representation of a Python object using JSON. You need a way to take an object and turn it into a JSON string. Here, I do this generically by defining a base class that records the constructor parameters and turns them into a JSON dictionary:

```
class Serializable(object):
    def __init__(self, *args):
        self.args = args

    def serialize(self):
        return json.dumps({'args': self.args})
```

This class makes it easy to serialize simple, immutable data structures like `Point2D` to a string.

```
class Point2D(Serializable):
    def __init__(self, x, y):
        super().__init__(x, y)
        self.x = x
        self.y = y

    def __repr__(self):
        return 'Point2D(%d, %d)' % (self.x, self.y)

point = Point2D(5, 3)
print('Object:    ', point)
print('Serialized:', point.serialize())

>>>
Object:     Point2D(5, 3)
Serialized: {"args": [5, 3]}
```

Now, I need to deserialize this JSON string and construct the Point2D object it represents. Here, I define another class that can deserialize the data from its Serializable parent class:

```
class Deserializable(Serializable):
    @classmethod
    def deserialize(cls, json_data):
        params = json.loads(json_data)
        return cls(*params['args'])
```

Using Deserializable makes it easy to serialize and deserialize simple, immutable objects in a generic way.

```
class BetterPoint2D(Deserializable):
    # ...

point = BetterPoint2D(5, 3)
print('Before:    ', point)
data = point.serialize()
print('Serialized:', data)
after = BetterPoint2D.deserialize(data)
print('After:     ', after)

>>>
Before:     BetterPoint2D(5, 3)
Serialized: {"args": [5, 3]}
After:      BetterPoint2D(5, 3)
```

The problem with this approach is that it only works if you know the intended type of the serialized data ahead of time (e.g., Point2D, BetterPoint2D). Ideally, you'd have a large number of classes serializing to JSON and one common function that could deserialize any of them back to a corresponding Python object.

To do this, I can include the serialized object's class name in the JSON data.

```
class BetterSerializable(object):
    def __init__(self, *args):
        self.args = args

    def serialize(self):
        return json.dumps({
            'class': self.__class__.__name__,
            'args': self.args,
        })

    def __repr__(self):
        # ...
```

Then, I can maintain a mapping of class names back to constructors for those objects. The general deserialize function will work for any classes passed to register_class.

```
registry = {}

def register_class(target_class):
    registry[target_class.__name__] = target_class

def deserialize(data):
    params = json.loads(data)
    name = params['class']
    target_class = registry[name]
    return target_class(*params['args'])
```

To ensure that deserialize always works properly, I must call register_class for every class I may want to deserialize in the future.

```
class EvenBetterPoint2D(BetterSerializable):
    def __init__(self, x, y):
        super().__init__(x, y)
        self.x = x
        self.y = y

register_class(EvenBetterPoint2D)
```

Now, I can deserialize an arbitrary JSON string without having to know which class it contains.

```
point = EvenBetterPoint2D(5, 3)
print('Before:    ', point)
data = point.serialize()
print('Serialized:', data)
after = deserialize(data)
print('After:     ', after)

>>>
Before:     EvenBetterPoint2D(5, 3)
Serialized: {"class": "EvenBetterPoint2D", "args": [5, 3]}
After:      EvenBetterPoint2D(5, 3)
```

The problem with this approach is that you can forget to call register_class.

```
class Point3D(BetterSerializable):
    def __init__(self, x, y, z):
        super().__init__(x, y, z)
        self.x = x
```

```
        self.y = y
        self.z = z

# Forgot to call register_class! Whoops!
```

This will cause your code to break at runtime, when you finally try to deserialize an object of a class you forgot to register.

```
point = Point3D(5, 9, -4)
data = point.serialize()
deserialize(data)

>>>
KeyError: 'Point3D'
```

Even though you chose to subclass `BetterSerializable`, you won't actually get all of its features if you forget to call `register_class` after your `class` statement body. This approach is error prone and especially challenging for beginners. The same omission can happen with *class decorators* in Python 3.

What if you could somehow act on the programmer's intent to use `BetterSerializable` and ensure that `register_class` is called in all cases? Metaclasses enable this by intercepting the `class` statement when subclasses are defined (see Item 33: "Validate Subclasses with Metaclasses"). This lets you register the new type immediately after the class's body.

```
class Meta(type):
    def __new__(meta, name, bases, class_dict):
        cls = type.__new__(meta, name, bases, class_dict)
        register_class(cls)
        return cls

class RegisteredSerializable(BetterSerializable,
                             metaclass=Meta):
    pass
```

When I define a subclass of `RegisteredSerializable`, I can be confident that the call to `register_class` happened and `deserialize` will always work as expected.

```
class Vector3D(RegisteredSerializable):
    def __init__(self, x, y, z):
        super().__init__(x, y, z)
        self.x, self.y, self.z = x, y, z

v3 = Vector3D(10, -7, 3)
print('Before:    ', v3)
```

```
data = v3.serialize()
print('Serialized:', data)
print('After:     ', deserialize(data))

>>>
Before:     Vector3D(10, -7, 3)
Serialized: {"class": "Vector3D", "args": [10, -7, 3]}
After:      Vector3D(10, -7, 3)
```

Using metaclasses for class registration ensures that you'll never miss a class as long as the inheritance tree is right. This works well for serialization, as I've shown, and also applies to database object-relationship mappings (ORMs), plug-in systems, and system hooks.

### Things to Remember

- ✦ Class registration is a helpful pattern for building modular Python programs.
- ✦ Metaclasses let you run registration code automatically each time your base class is subclassed in a program.
- ✦ Using metaclasses for class registration avoids errors by ensuring that you never miss a registration call.

## Item 35: Annotate Class Attributes with Metaclasses

One more useful feature enabled by metaclasses is the ability to modify or annotate properties after a class is defined but before the class is actually used. This approach is commonly used with *descriptors* (see Item 31: "Use Descriptors for Reusable `@property` Methods") to give them more introspection into how they're being used within their containing class.

For example, say you want to define a new class that represents a row in your customer database. You'd like a corresponding property on the class for each column in the database table. To do this, here I define a descriptor class to connect attributes to column names.

```
class Field(object):
    def __init__(self, name):
        self.name = name
        self.internal_name = '_' + self.name

    def __get__(self, instance, instance_type):
        if instance is None: return self
        return getattr(instance, self.internal_name, '')
```

```
    def __set__(self, instance, value):
        setattr(instance, self.internal_name, value)
```

With the column name stored in the Field descriptor, I can save all of the per-instance state directly in the instance dictionary as protected fields using the setattr and getattr built-in functions. At first, this seems to be much more convenient than building descriptors with weakref to avoid memory leaks.

Defining the class representing a row requires supplying the column name for each class attribute.

```
class Customer(object):
    # Class attributes
    first_name = Field('first_name')
    last_name = Field('last_name')
    prefix = Field('prefix')
    suffix = Field('suffix')
```

Using the class is simple. Here, you can see how the Field descriptors modify the instance dictionary __dict__ as expected:

```
foo = Customer()
print('Before:', repr(foo.first_name), foo.__dict__)
foo.first_name = 'Euclid'
print('After: ', repr(foo.first_name), foo.__dict__)

>>>
Before: '' {}
After:  'Euclid' {'_first_name': 'Euclid'}
```

But it seems redundant. I already declared the name of the field when I assigned the constructed Field object to Customer.first_name in the class statement body. Why do I also have to pass the field name ('first_name' in this case) to the Field constructor?

The problem is that the order of operations in the Customer class definition is the opposite of how it reads from left to right. First, the Field constructor is called as Field('first_name'). Then, the return value of that is assigned to Customer.field_name. There's no way for the Field to know upfront which class attribute it will be assigned to.

To eliminate the redundancy, I can use a metaclass. Metaclasses let you hook the class statement directly and take action as soon as a class body is finished. In this case, I can use the metaclass to assign Field.name and Field.internal_name on the descriptor automatically instead of manually specifying the field name multiple times.

```
class Meta(type):
    def __new__(meta, name, bases, class_dict):
        for key, value in class_dict.items():
            if isinstance(value, Field):
                value.name = key
                value.internal_name = '_' + key
        cls = type.__new__(meta, name, bases, class_dict)
        return cls
```

Here, I define a base class that uses the metaclass. All classes representing database rows should inherit from this class to ensure that they use the metaclass:

```
class DatabaseRow(object, metaclass=Meta):
    pass
```

To work with the metaclass, the field descriptor is largely unchanged. The only difference is that it no longer requires any arguments to be passed to its constructor. Instead, its attributes are set by the `Meta.__new__` method above.

```
class Field(object):
    def __init__(self):
        # These will be assigned by the metaclass.
        self.name = None
        self.internal_name = None
    # ...
```

By using the metaclass, the new `DatabaseRow` base class, and the new `Field` descriptor, the class definition for a database row no longer has the redundancy from before.

```
class BetterCustomer(DatabaseRow):
    first_name = Field()
    last_name = Field()
    prefix = Field()
    suffix = Field()
```

The behavior of the new class is identical to the old one.

```
foo = BetterCustomer()
print('Before:', repr(foo.first_name), foo.__dict__)
foo.first_name = 'Euler'
print('After: ', repr(foo.first_name), foo.__dict__)

>>>
Before: '' {}
After:  'Euler' {'_first_name': 'Euler'}
```

### Things to Remember

- ✦ Metaclasses enable you to modify a class's attributes before the class is fully defined.
- ✦ Descriptors and metaclasses make a powerful combination for declarative behavior and runtime introspection.
- ✦ You can avoid both memory leaks and the `weakref` module by using metaclasses along with descriptors.

# 5 Concurrency and Parallelism

Concurrency is when a computer does many different things *seemingly* at the same time. For example, on a computer with one CPU core, the operating system will rapidly change which program is running on the single processor. This interleaves execution of the programs, providing the illusion that the programs are running simultaneously.

Parallelism is *actually* doing many different things at the same time. Computers with multiple CPU cores can execute multiple programs simultaneously. Each CPU core runs the instructions of a separate program, allowing each program to make forward progress during the same instant.

Within a single program, concurrency is a tool that makes it easier for programmers to solve certain types of problems. Concurrent programs enable many distinct paths of execution to make forward progress in a way that seems to be both simultaneous and independent.

The key difference between parallelism and concurrency is *speedup*. When two distinct paths of execution in a program make forward progress in parallel, the time it takes to do the total work is cut in half; the speed of execution is faster by a factor of two. In contrast, concurrent programs may run thousands of separate paths of execution seemingly in parallel but provide no speedup for the total work.

Python makes it easy to write concurrent programs. Python can also be used to do parallel work through system calls, subprocesses, and C-extensions. But it can be very difficult to make concurrent Python code truly run in parallel. It's important to understand how to best utilize Python in these subtly different situations.

## Item 36: Use subprocess to Manage Child Processes

Python has battle-hardened libraries for running and managing child processes. This makes Python a great language for gluing other tools together, such as command-line utilities. When existing shell scripts get complicated, as they often do over time, graduating them to a rewrite in Python is a natural choice for the sake of readability and maintainability.

Child processes started by Python are able to run in parallel, enabling you to use Python to consume all of the CPU cores of your machine and maximize the throughput of your programs. Although Python itself may be CPU bound (see Item 37: "Use Threads for Blocking I/O, Avoid for Parallelism"), it's easy to use Python to drive and coordinate CPU-intensive workloads.

Python has had many ways to run subprocesses over the years, including `popen`, `popen2`, and `os.exec*`. With the Python of today, the best and simplest choice for managing child processes is to use the `subprocess` built-in module.

Running a child process with `subprocess` is simple. Here, the `Popen` constructor starts the process. The `communicate` method reads the child process's output and waits for termination.

```
proc = subprocess.Popen(
    ['echo', 'Hello from the child!'],
    stdout=subprocess.PIPE)
out, err = proc.communicate()
print(out.decode('utf-8'))

>>>
Hello from the child!
```

Child processes will run independently from their parent process, the Python interpreter. Their status can be polled periodically while Python does other work.

```
proc = subprocess.Popen(['sleep', '0.3'])
while proc.poll() is None:
    print('Working...')
    # Some time-consuming work here
    # ...

print('Exit status', proc.poll())

>>>
Working...
Working...
Exit status 0
```

Decoupling the child process from the parent means that the parent process is free to run many child processes in parallel. You can do this by starting all the child processes together upfront.

```
def run_sleep(period):
    proc = subprocess.Popen(['sleep', str(period)])
    return proc

start = time()
procs = []
for _ in range(10):
    proc = run_sleep(0.1)
    procs.append(proc)
```

Later, you can wait for them to finish their I/O and terminate with the communicate method.

```
for proc in procs:
    proc.communicate()
end = time()
print('Finished in %.3f seconds' % (end - start))

>>>
Finished in 0.117 seconds
```

> Note
>
> If these processes ran in sequence, the total delay would be 1 second, not the ~0.1 second I measured.

You can also pipe data from your Python program into a subprocess and retrieve its output. This allows you to utilize other programs to do work in parallel. For example, say you want to use the openssl command-line tool to encrypt some data. Starting the child process with command-line arguments and I/O pipes is easy.

```
def run_openssl(data):
    env = os.environ.copy()
    env['password'] = b'\xe24U\n\xd0Ql3S\x11'
    proc = subprocess.Popen(
        ['openssl', 'enc', '-des3', '-pass', 'env:password'],
        env=env,
        stdin=subprocess.PIPE,
        stdout=subprocess.PIPE)
    proc.stdin.write(data)
    proc.stdin.flush()  # Ensure the child gets input
    return proc
```

Here, I pipe random bytes into the encryption function, but in practice this would be user input, a file handle, a network socket, etc.:

```
procs = []
for _ in range(3):
    data = os.urandom(10)
    proc = run_openssl(data)
    procs.append(proc)
```

The child processes will run in parallel and consume their input. Here, I wait for them to finish and then retrieve their final output:

```
for proc in procs:
    out, err = proc.communicate()
    print(out[-10:])

>>>
b'o4,G\x91\x95\xfe\xa0\xaa\xb7'
b'\x0b\x01\\\xb1\xb7\xfb\xb2C\xe1b'
b'ds\xc5\xf4;j\x1f\xd0c-'
```

You can also create chains of parallel processes just like UNIX pipes, connecting the output of one child process into the input of another, and so on. Here's a function that starts a child process that will cause the md5 command-line tool to consume an input stream:

```
def run_md5(input_stdin):
    proc = subprocess.Popen(
        ['md5'],
        stdin=input_stdin,
        stdout=subprocess.PIPE)
    return proc
```

**Note**

Python's hashlib built-in module provides the md5 function, so running a subprocess like this isn't always necessary. The goal here is to demonstrate how subprocesses can pipe inputs and outputs.

Now, I can kick off a set of openssl processes to encrypt some data and another set of processes to md5 hash the encrypted output.

```
input_procs = []
hash_procs = []
for _ in range(3):
    data = os.urandom(10)
    proc = run_openssl(data)
    input_procs.append(proc)
    hash_proc = run_md5(proc.stdout)
    hash_procs.append(hash_proc)
```

The I/O between the child processes will happen automatically once you get them started. All you need to do is wait for them to finish and print the final output.

```
for proc in input_procs:
    proc.communicate()
for proc in hash_procs:
    out, err = proc.communicate()
    print(out.strip())

>>>
b'7a1822875dcf9650a5a71e5e41e77bf3'
b'd41d8cd98f00b204e9800998ecf8427e'
b'1720f581cfdc448b6273048d42621100'
```

If you're worried about the child processes never finishing or somehow blocking on input or output pipes, then be sure to pass the `timeout` parameter to the `communicate` method. This will cause an exception to be raised if the child process hasn't responded within a time period, giving you a chance to terminate the misbehaving child.

```
proc = run_sleep(10)
try:
    proc.communicate(timeout=0.1)
except subprocess.TimeoutExpired:
    proc.terminate()
    proc.wait()

print('Exit status', proc.poll())

>>>
Exit status -15
```

Unfortunately, the `timeout` parameter is only available in Python 3.3 and later. In earlier versions of Python, you'll need to use the `select` built-in module on `proc.stdin`, `proc.stdout`, and `proc.stderr` in order to enforce timeouts on I/O.

### Things to Remember

- ✦ Use the `subprocess` module to run child processes and manage their input and output streams.
- ✦ Child processes run in parallel with the Python interpreter, enabling you to maximize your CPU usage.
- ✦ Use the `timeout` parameter with `communicate` to avoid deadlocks and hanging child processes.

## Item 37: Use Threads for Blocking I/O, Avoid for Parallelism

The standard implementation of Python is called CPython. CPython runs a Python program in two steps. First, it parses and compiles the source text into bytecode. Then, it runs the bytecode using a stack-based interpreter. The bytecode interpreter has state that must be maintained and coherent while the Python program executes. Python enforces coherence with a mechanism called the *global interpreter lock* (GIL).

Essentially, the GIL is a mutual-exclusion lock (mutex) that prevents CPython from being affected by preemptive multithreading, where one thread takes control of a program by interrupting another thread. Such an interruption could corrupt the interpreter state if it comes at an unexpected time. The GIL prevents these interruptions and ensures that every bytecode instruction works correctly with the CPython implementation and its C-extension modules.

The GIL has an important negative side effect. With programs written in languages like C++ or Java, having multiple threads of execution means your program could utilize multiple CPU cores at the same time. Although Python supports multiple threads of execution, the GIL causes only one of them to make forward progress at a time. This means that when you reach for threads to do parallel computation and speed up your Python programs, you will be sorely disappointed.

For example, say you want to do something computationally intensive with Python. I'll use a naive number factorization algorithm as a proxy.

```
def factorize(number):
    for i in range(1, number + 1):
        if number % i == 0:
            yield i
```

Factoring a set of numbers in serial takes quite a long time.

```
numbers = [2139079, 1214759, 1516637, 1852285]
start = time()
for number in numbers:
    list(factorize(number))
end = time()
print('Took %.3f seconds' % (end - start))

>>>
Took 1.040 seconds
```

Using multiple threads to do this computation would make sense in other languages because you could take advantage of all of the CPU cores of your computer. Let me try that in Python. Here, I define a Python thread for doing the same computation as before:

```
from threading import Thread


class FactorizeThread(Thread):
    def __init__(self, number):
        super().__init__()
        self.number = number

    def run(self):
        self.factors = list(factorize(self.number))
```

Then, I start a thread for factorizing each number in parallel.

```
start = time()
threads = []
for number in numbers:
    thread = FactorizeThread(number)
    thread.start()
    threads.append(thread)
```

Finally, I wait for all of the threads to finish.

```
for thread in threads:
    thread.join()
end = time()
print('Took %.3f seconds' % (end - start))

>>>
Took 1.061 seconds
```

What's surprising is that this takes even longer than running `factorize` in serial. With one thread per number, you may expect less than a 4× speedup in other languages due to the overhead of creating threads and coordinating with them. You may expect only a 2× speedup on the dual-core machine I used to run this code. But you would never expect the performance of these threads to be worse when you have multiple CPUs to utilize. This demonstrates the effect of the GIL on programs running in the standard CPython interpreter.

There are ways to get CPython to utilize multiple cores, but it doesn't work with the standard `Thread` class (see Item 41: "Consider `concurrent.futures` for True Parallelism") and it can require substantial effort. Knowing these limitations you may wonder, why does Python support threads at all? There are two good reasons.

First, multiple threads make it easy for your program to seem like it's doing multiple things at the same time. Managing the juggling act of simultaneous tasks is difficult to implement yourself (see Item 40: "Consider Coroutines to Run Many Functions Concurrently" for an example). With threads, you can leave it to Python to run your functions seemingly in parallel. This works because CPython ensures a level of fairness between Python threads of execution, even though only one of them makes forward progress at a time due to the GIL.

The second reason Python supports threads is to deal with blocking I/O, which happens when Python does certain types of system calls. System calls are how your Python program asks your computer's operating system to interact with the external environment on your behalf. Blocking I/O includes things like reading and writing files, interacting with networks, communicating with devices like displays, etc. Threads help you handle blocking I/O by insulating your program from the time it takes for the operating system to respond to your requests.

For example, say you want to send a signal to a remote-controlled helicopter through a serial port. I'll use a slow system call (`select`) as a proxy for this activity. This function asks the operating system to block for 0.1 second and then return control to my program, similar to what would happen when using a synchronous serial port.

```
import select

def slow_systemcall():
    select.select([], [], [], 0.1)
```

Running this system call in serial requires a linearly increasing amount of time.

```
start = time()
for _ in range(5):
    slow_systemcall()
end = time()
print('Took %.3f seconds' % (end - start))

>>>
Took 0.503 seconds
```

The problem is that while the `slow_systemcall` function is running, my program can't make any other progress. My program's main thread of execution is blocked on the `select` system call. This situation is awful in practice. You need to be able to compute your helicopter's next move while you're sending it a signal, otherwise it'll crash. When you find yourself needing to do blocking I/O and computation simultaneously, it's time to consider moving your system calls to threads.

Here, I run multiple invocations of the slow_systemcall function in separate threads. This would allow you to communicate with multiple serial ports (and helicopters) at the same time, while leaving the main thread to do whatever computation is required.

```
start = time()
threads = []
for _ in range(5):
    thread = Thread(target=slow_systemcall)
    thread.start()
    threads.append(thread)
```

With the threads started, here I do some work to calculate the next helicopter move before waiting for the system call threads to finish.

```
def compute_helicopter_location(index):
    # ...

for i in range(5):
    compute_helicopter_location(i)
for thread in threads:
    thread.join()
end = time()
print('Took %.3f seconds' % (end - start))

>>>
Took 0.102 seconds
```

The parallel time is 5× less than the serial time. This shows that the system calls will all run in parallel from multiple Python threads even though they're limited by the GIL. The GIL prevents my Python code from running in parallel, but it has no negative effect on system calls. This works because Python threads release the GIL just before they make system calls and reacquire the GIL as soon as the system calls are done.

There are many other ways to deal with blocking I/O besides threads, such as the asyncio built-in module, and these alternatives have important benefits. But these options also require extra work in refactoring your code to fit a different model of execution (see Item 40: "Consider Coroutines to Run Many Functions Concurrently"). Using threads is the simplest way to do blocking I/O in parallel with minimal changes to your program.

### Things to Remember

- ✦ Python threads can't run bytecode in parallel on multiple CPU cores because of the global interpreter lock (GIL).

- ✦ Python threads are still useful despite the GIL because they provide an easy way to do multiple things at seemingly the same time.
- ✦ Use Python threads to make multiple system calls in parallel. This allows you to do blocking I/O at the same time as computation.

## Item 38: Use Lock to Prevent Data Races in Threads

After learning about the global interpreter lock (GIL) (see Item 37: "Use Threads for Blocking I/O, Avoid for Parallelism"), many new Python programmers assume they can forgo using mutual-exclusion locks (mutexes) in their code altogether. If the GIL is already preventing Python threads from running on multiple CPU cores in parallel, it must also act as a lock for a program's data structures, right? Some testing on types like lists and dictionaries may even show that this assumption appears to hold.

But beware, this is truly not the case. The GIL will not protect you. Although only one Python thread runs at a time, a thread's operations on data structures can be interrupted between any two bytecode instructions in the Python interpreter. This is dangerous if you access the same objects from multiple threads simultaneously. The invariants of your data structures could be violated at practically any time because of these interruptions, leaving your program in a corrupted state.

For example, say you want to write a program that counts many things in parallel, like sampling light levels from a whole network of sensors. If you want to determine the total number of light samples over time, you can aggregate them with a new class.

```
class Counter(object):
    def __init__(self):
        self.count = 0

    def increment(self, offset):
        self.count += offset
```

Imagine that each sensor has its own worker thread because reading from the sensor requires blocking I/O. After each sensor measurement, the worker thread increments the counter up to a maximum number of desired readings.

```
def worker(sensor_index, how_many, counter):
    for _ in range(how_many):
        # Read from the sensor
        # ...
        counter.increment(1)
```

Here, I define a function that starts a worker thread for each sensor and waits for them all to finish their readings:

```
def run_threads(func, how_many, counter):
    threads = []
    for i in range(5):
        args = (i, how_many, counter)
        thread = Thread(target=func, args=args)
        threads.append(thread)
        thread.start()
    for thread in threads:
        thread.join()
```

Running five threads in parallel seems simple, and the outcome should be obvious.

```
how_many = 10**5
counter = Counter()
run_threads(worker, how_many, counter)
print('Counter should be %d, found %d' %
      (5 * how_many, counter.count))

>>>
Counter should be 500000, found 278328
```

But this result is way off! What happened here? How could something so simple go so wrong, especially since only one Python interpreter thread can run at a time?

The Python interpreter enforces fairness between all of the threads that are executing to ensure they get a roughly equal amount of processing time. To do this, Python will suspend a thread as it's running and will resume another thread in turn. The problem is that you don't know exactly when Python will suspend your threads. A thread can even be paused seemingly halfway through what looks like an atomic operation. That's what happened in this case.

The `Counter` object's `increment` method looks simple.

```
counter.count += offset
```

But the += operator used on an object attribute actually instructs Python to do three separate operations behind the scenes. The statement above is equivalent to this:

```
value = getattr(counter, 'count')
result = value + offset
setattr(counter, 'count', result)
```

Python threads incrementing the counter can be suspended between any two of these operations. This is problematic if the way the operations interleave causes old versions of value to be assigned to the counter. Here's an example of bad interaction between two threads, A and B:

```
# Running in Thread A
value_a = getattr(counter, 'count')
# Context switch to Thread B
value_b = getattr(counter, 'count')
result_b = value_b + 1
setattr(counter, 'count', result_b)
# Context switch back to Thread A
result_a = value_a + 1
setattr(counter, 'count', result_a)
```

Thread A stomped on thread B, erasing all of its progress incrementing the counter. This is exactly what happened in the light sensor example above.

To prevent data races like these and other forms of data structure corruption, Python includes a robust set of tools in the threading built-in module. The simplest and most useful of them is the Lock class, a mutual-exclusion lock (mutex).

By using a lock, I can have the Counter class protect its current value against simultaneous access from multiple threads. Only one thread will be able to acquire the lock at a time. Here, I use a with statement to acquire and release the lock; this makes it easier to see which code is executing while the lock is held (see Item 43: "Consider contextlib and with Statements for Reusable try/finally Behavior" for details):

```
class LockingCounter(object):
    def __init__(self):
        self.lock = Lock()
        self.count = 0

    def increment(self, offset):
        with self.lock:
            self.count += offset
```

Now I run the worker threads as before, but use a LockingCounter instead.

```
counter = LockingCounter()
run_threads(worker, how_many, counter)
print('Counter should be %d, found %d' %
      (5 * how_many, counter.count))
```

```
>>>
Counter should be 500000, found 500000
```

The result is exactly what I expect. The `Lock` solved the problem.

### Things to Remember

- ✦ Even though Python has a global interpreter lock, you're still responsible for protecting against data races between the threads in your programs.
- ✦ Your programs will corrupt their data structures if you allow multiple threads to modify the same objects without locks.
- ✦ The `Lock` class in the `threading` built-in module is Python's standard mutual exclusion lock implementation.

## Item 39: Use Queue to Coordinate Work Between Threads

Python programs that do many things concurrently often need to coordinate their work. One of the most useful arrangements for concurrent work is a pipeline of functions.

A pipeline works like an assembly line used in manufacturing. Pipelines have many phases in serial with a specific function for each phase. New pieces of work are constantly added to the beginning of the pipeline. Each function can operate concurrently on the piece of work in its phase. The work moves forward as each function completes until there are no phases remaining. This approach is especially good for work that includes blocking I/O or subprocesses—activities that can easily be parallelized using Python (see Item 37: "Use Threads for Blocking I/O, Avoid for Parallelism").

For example, say you want to build a system that will take a constant stream of images from your digital camera, resize them, and then add them to a photo gallery online. Such a program could be split into three phases of a pipeline. New images are retrieved in the first phase. The downloaded images are passed through the resize function in the second phase. The resized images are consumed by the upload function in the final phase.

Imagine you had already written Python functions that execute the phases: `download`, `resize`, `upload`. How do you assemble a pipeline to do the work concurrently?

The first thing you need is a way to hand off work between the pipeline phases. This can be modeled as a thread-safe producer-consumer queue (see Item 38: "Use Lock to Prevent Data Races in Threads" to understand the importance of thread safety in Python; see Item 46: "Use Built-in Algorithms and Data Structures" for the deque class).

```
class MyQueue(object):
    def __init__(self):
        self.items = deque()
        self.lock = Lock()
```

The producer, your digital camera, adds new images to the end of the list of pending items.

```
    def put(self, item):
        with self.lock:
            self.items.append(item)
```

The consumer, the first phase of your processing pipeline, removes images from the front of the list of pending items.

```
    def get(self):
        with self.lock:
            return self.items.popleft()
```

Here, I represent each phase of the pipeline as a Python thread that takes work from one queue like this, runs a function on it, and puts the result on another queue. I also track how many times the worker has checked for new input and how much work it's completed.

```
class Worker(Thread):
    def __init__(self, func, in_queue, out_queue):
        super().__init__()
        self.func = func
        self.in_queue = in_queue
        self.out_queue = out_queue
        self.polled_count = 0
        self.work_done = 0
```

The trickiest part is that the worker thread must properly handle the case where the input queue is empty because the previous phase hasn't completed its work yet. This happens where I catch the IndexError exception below. You can think of this as a holdup in the assembly line.

```
    def run(self):
        while True:
            self.polled_count += 1
            try:
                item = self.in_queue.get()
            except IndexError:
                sleep(0.01)  # No work to do
```

```
        else:
            result = self.func(item)
            self.out_queue.put(result)
            self.work_done += 1
```

Now I can connect the three phases together by creating the queues for their coordination points and the corresponding worker threads.

```
download_queue = MyQueue()
resize_queue = MyQueue()
upload_queue = MyQueue()
done_queue = MyQueue()
threads = [
    Worker(download, download_queue, resize_queue),
    Worker(resize, resize_queue, upload_queue),
    Worker(upload, upload_queue, done_queue),
]
```

I can start the threads and then inject a bunch of work into the first phase of the pipeline. Here, I use a plain `object` instance as a proxy for the real data required by the `download` function:

```
for thread in threads:
    thread.start()
for _ in range(1000):
    download_queue.put(object())
```

Now I wait for all of the items to be processed by the pipeline and end up in the `done_queue`.

```
while len(done_queue.items) < 1000:
    # Do something useful while waiting
    # ...
```

This runs properly, but there's an interesting side effect caused by the threads polling their input queues for new work. The tricky part, where I catch `IndexError` exceptions in the `run` method, executes a large number of times.

```
processed = len(done_queue.items)
polled = sum(t.polled_count for t in threads)
print('Processed', processed, 'items after polling',
      polled, 'times')

>>>
Processed 1000 items after polling 3030 times
```

When the worker functions vary in speeds, an earlier phase can prevent progress in later phases, backing up the pipeline. This causes later phases to starve and constantly check their input queues for new work in a tight loop. The outcome is that worker threads waste CPU time doing nothing useful (they're constantly raising and catching IndexError exceptions).

But that's just the beginning of what's wrong with this implementation. There are three more problems that you should also avoid. First, determining that all of the input work is complete requires yet another busy wait on the done_queue. Second, in Worker the run method will execute forever in its busy loop. There's no way to signal to a worker thread that it's time to exit.

Third, and worst of all, a backup in the pipeline can cause the program to crash arbitrarily. If the first phase makes rapid progress but the second phase makes slow progress, then the queue connecting the first phase to the second phase will constantly increase in size. The second phase won't be able to keep up. Given enough time and input data, the program will eventually run out of memory and die.

The lesson here isn't that pipelines are bad; it's that it's hard to build a good producer-consumer queue yourself.

### Queue to the Rescue

The Queue class from the queue built-in module provides all of the functionality you need to solve these problems.

Queue eliminates the busy waiting in the worker by making the get method block until new data is available. For example, here I start a thread that waits for some input data on a queue:

```
from queue import Queue
queue = Queue()

def consumer():
    print('Consumer waiting')
    queue.get()                # Runs after put() below
    print('Consumer done')

thread = Thread(target=consumer)
thread.start()
```

Even though the thread is running first, it won't finish until an item is put on the Queue instance and the get method has something to return.

```
print('Producer putting')
queue.put(object())            # Runs before get() above
thread.join()
print('Producer done')
```

```
>>>
Consumer waiting
Producer putting
Consumer done
Producer done
```

To solve the pipeline backup issue, the `Queue` class lets you specify the maximum amount of pending work you'll allow between two phases. This buffer size causes calls to `put` to block when the queue is already full. For example, here I define a thread that waits for a while before consuming a queue:

```
queue = Queue(1)                # Buffer size of 1

def consumer():
    time.sleep(0.1)             # Wait
    queue.get()                 # Runs second
    print('Consumer got 1')
    queue.get()                 # Runs fourth
    print('Consumer got 2')

thread = Thread(target=consumer)
thread.start()
```

The wait should allow the producer thread to `put` both objects on the queue before the `consume` thread ever calls `get`. But the `Queue` size is one. That means the producer adding items to the queue will have to wait for the consumer thread to call `get` at least once before the second call to `put` will stop blocking and add the second item to the queue.

```
queue.put(object())             # Runs first
print('Producer put 1')
queue.put(object())             # Runs third
print('Producer put 2')
thread.join()
print('Producer done')

>>>
Producer put 1
Consumer got 1
Producer put 2
Consumer got 2
Producer done
```

The `Queue` class can also track the progress of work using the `task_done` method. This lets you wait for a phase's input queue to drain and eliminates the need for polling the done_queue at the end of your pipeline. For example, here I define a consumer thread that calls task_done when it finishes working on an item.

```
in_queue = Queue()


def consumer():
    print('Consumer waiting')
    work = in_queue.get()          # Done second
    print('Consumer working')
    # Doing work
    # ...
    print('Consumer done')
    in_queue.task_done()           # Done third

Thread(target=consumer).start()
```

Now, the producer code doesn't have to join the consumer thread or poll. The producer can just wait for the in_queue to finish by calling join on the Queue instance. Even once it's empty, the in_queue won't be joinable until after task_done is called for every item that was ever enqueued.

```
in_queue.put(object())             # Done first
print('Producer waiting')
in_queue.join()                    # Done fourth
print('Producer done')

>>>
Consumer waiting
Producer waiting
Consumer working
Consumer done
Producer done
```

I can put all of these behaviors together into a Queue subclass that also tells the worker thread when it should stop processing. Here, I define a close method that adds a special item to the queue that indicates there will be no more input items after it:

```
class ClosableQueue(Queue):
    SENTINEL = object()

    def close(self):
        self.put(self.SENTINEL)
```

Then, I define an iterator for the queue that looks for this special object and stops iteration when it's found. This `__iter__` method also calls `task_done` at appropriate times, letting me track the progress of work on the queue.

```
    def __iter__(self):
        while True:
            item = self.get()
            try:
                if item is self.SENTINEL:
                    return  # Cause the thread to exit
                yield item
            finally:
                self.task_done()
```

Now, I can redefine my worker thread to rely on the behavior of the `ClosableQueue` class. The thread will exit once the for loop is exhausted.

```
class StoppableWorker(Thread):
    def __init__(self, func, in_queue, out_queue):
        # ...

    def run(self):
        for item in self.in_queue:
            result = self.func(item)
            self.out_queue.put(result)
```

Here, I re-create the set of worker threads using the new worker class:

```
download_queue = ClosableQueue()
# ...
threads = [
    StoppableWorker(download, download_queue, resize_queue),
    # ...
]
```

After running the worker threads like before, I also send the stop signal once all the input work has been injected by closing the input queue of the first phase.

```
for thread in threads:
    thread.start()
for _ in range(1000):
    download_queue.put(object())
download_queue.close()
```

Finally, I wait for the work to finish by joining each queue that connects the phases. Each time one phase is done, I signal the next phase to stop by closing its input queue. At the end, the done_queue contains all of the output objects as expected.

```
download_queue.join()
resize_queue.close()
resize_queue.join()
upload_queue.close()
upload_queue.join()
print(done_queue.qsize(), 'items finished')

>>>
1000 items finished
```

### Things to Remember

- ✦ Pipelines are a great way to organize sequences of work that run concurrently using multiple Python threads.
- ✦ Be aware of the many problems in building concurrent pipelines: busy waiting, stopping workers, and memory explosion.
- ✦ The Queue class has all of the facilities you need to build robust pipelines: blocking operations, buffer sizes, and joining.

## Item 40: Consider Coroutines to Run Many Functions Concurrently

Threads give Python programmers a way to run multiple functions seemingly at the same time (see Item 37: "Use Threads for Blocking I/O, Avoid for Parallelism"). But there are three big problems with threads:

- They require special tools to coordinate with each other safely (see Item 38: "Use Lock to Prevent Data Races in Threads" and Item 39: "Use Queue to Coordinate Work Between Threads"). This makes code that uses threads harder to reason about than procedural, single-threaded code. This complexity makes threaded code more difficult to extend and maintain over time.
- Threads require a lot of memory, about 8 MB per executing thread. On many computers, that amount of memory doesn't matter for a dozen threads or so. But what if you want your program to run tens of thousands of functions "simultaneously"? These functions may correspond to user requests to a server, pixels on a screen, particles in a simulation, etc. Running a thread per unique activity just won't work.
- Threads are costly to start. If you want to constantly be creating new concurrent functions and finishing them, the overhead of using threads becomes large and slows everything down.

Python can work around all these issues with *coroutines*. Coroutines let you have many seemingly simultaneous functions in your Python programs. They're implemented as an extension to generators (see Item 16: "Consider Generators Instead of Returning Lists"). The cost of starting a generator coroutine is a function call. Once active, they each use less than 1 KB of memory until they're exhausted.

Coroutines work by enabling the code consuming a generator to `send` a value back into the generator function after each `yield` expression. The generator function receives the value passed to the `send` function as the result of the corresponding `yield` expression.

```
def my_coroutine():
    while True:
        received = yield
        print('Received:', received)

it = my_coroutine()
next(it)            # Prime the coroutine
it.send('First')
it.send('Second')

>>>
Received: First
Received: Second
```

The initial call to `next` is required to prepare the generator for receiving the first `send` by advancing it to the first `yield` expression. Together, `yield` and `send` provide generators with a standard way to vary their next yielded value in response to external input.

For example, say you want to implement a generator coroutine that yields the minimum value it's been sent so far. Here, the bare `yield` prepares the coroutine with the initial minimum value sent in from the outside. Then the generator repeatedly yields the new minimum in exchange for the next value to consider.

```
def minimize():
    current = yield
    while True:
        value = yield current
        current = min(value, current)
```

The code consuming the generator can run one step at a time and will output the minimum value seen after each input.

```
it = minimize()
next(it)            # Prime the generator
print(it.send(10))
```

```
print(it.send(4))
print(it.send(22))
print(it.send(-1))

>>>
10
4
4
-1
```

The generator function will seemingly run forever, making forward progress with each new call to `send`. Like threads, coroutines are independent functions that can consume inputs from their environment and produce resulting outputs. The difference is that coroutines pause at each `yield` expression in the generator function and resume after each call to `send` from the outside. This is the magical mechanism of coroutines.

This behavior allows the code consuming the generator to take action after each `yield` expression in the coroutine. The consuming code can use the generator's output values to call other functions and update data structures. Most importantly, it can advance other generator functions until their next `yield` expressions. By advancing many separate generators in lockstep, they will all seem to be running simultaneously, mimicking the concurrent behavior of Python threads.

### The Game of Life

Let me demonstrate the simultaneous behavior of coroutines with an example. Say you want to use coroutines to implement Conway's Game of Life. The rules of the game are simple. You have a two-dimensional grid of an arbitrary size. Each cell in the grid can either be alive or empty.

```
ALIVE = '*'
EMPTY = '-'
```

The game progresses one tick of the clock at a time. At each tick, each cell counts how many of its neighboring eight cells are still alive. Based on its neighbor count, each cell decides if it will keep living, die, or regenerate. Here's an example of a 5×5 Game of Life grid after four generations with time going to the right. I'll explain the specific rules further below.

```
  0   |   1   |   2   |   3   |   4
----- | ----- | ----- | ----- | -----
-*--- | --*-- | --**- | --*-- | -----
--**- | --**- | -*--- | -*--- | -**--
---*- | --**- | --**- | --*-- | -----
----- | ----- | ----- | ----- | -----
```

I can model this game by representing each cell as a generator coroutine running in lockstep with all the others.

To implement this, first I need a way to retrieve the status of neighboring cells. I can do this with a coroutine named `count_neighbors` that works by yielding `Query` objects. The `Query` class I define myself. Its purpose is to provide the generator coroutine with a way to ask its surrounding environment for information.

```
Query = namedtuple('Query', ('y', 'x'))
```

The coroutine yields a `Query` for each neighbor. The result of each `yield` expression will be the value `ALIVE` or `EMPTY`. That's the interface contract I've defined between the coroutine and its consuming code. The `count_neighbors` generator sees the neighbors' states and returns the count of living neighbors.

```
def count_neighbors(y, x):
    n_ = yield Query(y + 1, x + 0) # North
    ne = yield Query(y + 1, x + 1)  # Northeast
    # Define e_, se, s_, sw, w_, nw ...
    # ...
    neighbor_states = [n_, ne, e_, se, s_, sw, w_, nw]
    count = 0
    for state in neighbor_states:
        if state == ALIVE:
            count += 1
    return count
```

I can drive the `count_neighbors` coroutine with fake data to test it. Here, I show how `Query` objects will be yielded for each neighbor. `count_neighbors` expects to receive cell states corresponding to each `Query` through the coroutine's `send` method. The final count is returned in the `StopIteration` exception that is raised when the generator is exhausted by the `return` statement.

```
it = count_neighbors(10, 5)
q1 = next(it)                  # Get the first query
print('First yield: ', q1)
q2 = it.send(ALIVE)            # Send q1 state, get q2
print('Second yield:', q2)
q3 = it.send(ALIVE)            # Send q2 state, get q3
# ...
try:
    count = it.send(EMPTY)     # Send q8 state, retrieve count
except StopIteration as e:
    print('Count: ', e.value)  # Value from return statement
```

```
>>>
First yield:  Query(y=11, x=5)
Second yield: Query(y=11, x=6)
...
Count:  2
```

Now I need the ability to indicate that a cell will transition to a new state in response to the neighbor count that it found from `count_neighbors`. To do this, I define another coroutine called `step_cell`. This generator will indicate transitions in a cell's state by yielding `Transition` objects. This is another class that I define, just like the `Query` class.

```
Transition = namedtuple('Transition', ('y', 'x', 'state'))
```

The `step_cell` coroutine receives its coordinates in the grid as arguments. It yields a `Query` to get the initial state of those coordinates. It runs `count_neighbors` to inspect the cells around it. It runs the game logic to determine what state the cell should have for the next clock tick. Finally, it yields a `Transition` object to tell the environment the cell's next state.

```
def game_logic(state, neighbors):
    # ...

def step_cell(y, x):
    state = yield Query(y, x)
    neighbors = yield from count_neighbors(y, x)
    next_state = game_logic(state, neighbors)
    yield Transition(y, x, next_state)
```

Importantly, the call to `count_neighbors` uses the `yield from` expression. This expression allows Python to compose generator coroutines together, making it easy to reuse smaller pieces of functionality and build complex coroutines from simpler ones. When `count_neighbors` is exhausted, the final value it returns (with the `return` statement) will be passed to `step_cell` as the result of the `yield from` expression.

Now, I can finally define the simple game logic for Conway's Game of Life. There are only three rules.

```
def game_logic(state, neighbors):
    if state == ALIVE:
        if neighbors < 2:
            return EMPTY     # Die: Too few
        elif neighbors > 3:
            return EMPTY     # Die: Too many
    else:
        if neighbors == 3:
            return ALIVE     # Regenerate
    return state
```

I can drive the step_cell coroutine with fake data to test it.

```
it = step_cell(10, 5)
q0 = next(it)              # Initial location query
print('Me:      ', q0)
q1 = it.send(ALIVE)        # Send my status, get neighbor query
print('Q1:      ', q1)
# ...
t1 = it.send(EMPTY)        # Send for q8, get game decision
print('Outcome: ', t1)

>>>
Me:       Query(y=10, x=5)
Q1:       Query(y=11, x=5)
...
Outcome:  Transition(y=10, x=5, state='-')
```

The goal of the game is to run this logic for a whole grid of cells in lockstep. To do this, I can further compose the step_cell coroutine into a simulate coroutine. This coroutine progresses the grid of cells forward by yielding from step_cell many times. After progressing every coordinate, it yields a TICK object to indicate that the current generation of cells have all transitioned.

```
TICK = object()

def simulate(height, width):
    while True:
        for y in range(height):
            for x in range(width):
                yield from step_cell(y, x)
        yield TICK
```

What's impressive about simulate is that it's completely disconnected from the surrounding environment. I still haven't defined how the grid is represented in Python objects, how Query, Transition, and TICK values are handled on the outside, nor how the game gets its initial state. But the logic is clear. Each cell will transition by running step_cell. Then the game clock will tick. This will continue forever, as long as the simulate coroutine is advanced.

This is the beauty of coroutines. They help you focus on the logic of what you're trying to accomplish. They decouple your code's instructions for the environment from the implementation that carries out your wishes. This enables you to run coroutines seemingly in parallel. This also allows you to improve the implementation of following those instructions over time without changing the coroutines.

Now, I want to run simulate in a real environment. To do that, I need to represent the state of each cell in the grid. Here, I define a class to contain the grid:

```
class Grid(object):
    def __init__(self, height, width):
        self.height = height
        self.width = width
        self.rows = []
        for _ in range(self.height):
            self.rows.append([EMPTY] * self.width)

    def __str__(self):
        # ...
```

The grid allows you to get and set the value of any coordinate. Coordinates that are out of bounds will wrap around, making the grid act like infinite looping space.

```
    def query(self, y, x):
        return self.rows[y % self.height][x % self.width]

    def assign(self, y, x, state):
        self.rows[y % self.height][x % self.width] = state
```

At last, I can define the function that interprets the values yielded from simulate and all of its interior coroutines. This function turns the instructions from the coroutines into interactions with the surrounding environment. It progresses the whole grid of cells forward a single step and then returns a new grid containing the next state.

```
def live_a_generation(grid, sim):
    progeny = Grid(grid.height, grid.width)
    item = next(sim)
    while item is not TICK:
        if isinstance(item, Query):
            state = grid.query(item.y, item.x)
            item = sim.send(state)
        else:  # Must be a Transition
            progeny.assign(item.y, item.x, item.state)
            item = next(sim)
    return progeny
```

To see this function in action, I need to create a grid and set its initial state. Here, I make a classic shape called a glider.

```
grid = Grid(5, 9)
grid.assign(0, 3, ALIVE)
# ...
print(grid)

>>>
---*-----
----*----
--***----
---------
---------
```

Now I can progress this grid forward one generation at a time. You can see how the glider moves down and to the right on the grid based on the simple rules from the game_logic function.

```
class ColumnPrinter(object):
    # ...


columns = ColumnPrinter()
sim = simulate(grid.height, grid.width)
for i in range(5):
    columns.append(str(grid))
    grid = live_a_generation(grid, sim)

print(columns)

>>>
    0     |     1     |     2     |     3     |     4
---*----- | --------- | --------- | --------- | ---------
----*---- | --*-*---- | ----*---- | ---*----- | ----*----
--***---- | ---**---- | --*-*---- | ----**--- | -----*---
--------- | ---*----- | ---**---- | ---**---- | ---***---
--------- | --------- | --------- | --------- | ---------
```

The best part about this approach is that I can change the game_logic function without having to update the code that surrounds it. I can change the rules or add larger spheres of influence with the existing mechanics of Query, Transition, and TICK. This demonstrates how coroutines enable the separation of concerns, which is an important design principle.

## Coroutines in Python 2

Unfortunately, Python 2 is missing some of the syntactical sugar that makes coroutines so elegant in Python 3. There are two limitations.

First, there is no yield from expression. That means that when you want to compose generator coroutines in Python 2, you need to include an additional loop at the delegation point.

```
# Python 2
def delegated():
    yield 1
    yield 2

def composed():
    yield 'A'
    for value in delegated():  # yield from in Python 3
        yield value
    yield 'B'

print list(composed())

>>>
['A', 1, 2, 'B']
```

The second limitation is that there is no support for the return statement in Python 2 generators. To get the same behavior that interacts correctly with try/except/finally blocks, you need to define your own exception type and raise it when you want to return a value.

```
# Python 2
class MyReturn(Exception):
    def __init__(self, value):
        self.value = value

def delegated():
    yield 1
    raise MyReturn(2)  # return 2 in Python 3
    yield 'Not reached'

def composed():
    try:
        for value in delegated():
            yield value
    except MyReturn as e:
        output = e.value
    yield output * 4

print list(composed())

>>>
[1, 8]
```

### Things to Remember

- ✦ Coroutines provide an efficient way to run tens of thousands of functions seemingly at the same time.
- ✦ Within a generator, the value of the `yield` expression will be whatever value was passed to the generator's `send` method from the exterior code.
- ✦ Coroutines give you a powerful tool for separating the core logic of your program from its interaction with the surrounding environment.
- ✦ Python 2 doesn't support `yield from` or returning values from generators.

## Item 41: Consider `concurrent.futures` for True Parallelism

At some point in writing Python programs, you may hit the performance wall. Even after optimizing your code (see Item 58: "Profile Before Optimizing"), your program's execution may still be too slow for your needs. On modern computers that have an increasing number of CPU cores, it's reasonable to assume that one solution would be parallelism. What if you could split your code's computation into independent pieces of work that run simultaneously across multiple CPU cores?

Unfortunately, Python's global interpreter lock (GIL) prevents true parallelism in threads (see Item 37: "Use Threads for Blocking I/O, Avoid for Parallelism"), so that option is out. Another common suggestion is to rewrite your most performance-critical code as an extension module using the C language. C gets you closer to the bare metal and can run faster than Python, eliminating the need for parallelism. C-extensions can also start native threads that run in parallel and utilize multiple CPU cores. Python's API for C-extensions is well documented and a good choice for an escape hatch.

But rewriting your code in C has a high cost. Code that is short and understandable in Python can become verbose and complicated in C. Such a port requires extensive testing to ensure that the functionality is equivalent to the original Python code and that no bugs have been introduced. Sometimes it's worth it, which explains the large ecosystem of C-extension modules in the Python community that speed up things like text parsing, image compositing, and matrix math. There are even open source tools such as Cython (http://cython.org/) and Numba (http://numba.pydata.org/) that can ease the transition to C.

The problem is that moving one piece of your program to C isn't sufficient most of the time. Optimized Python programs usually don't have one major source of slowness, but rather, there are often many significant contributors. To get the benefits of C's bare metal and threads, you'd need to port large parts of your program, drastically increasing testing needs and risk. There must be a better way to preserve your investment in Python to solve difficult computational problems.

The `multiprocessing` built-in module, easily accessed via the `concurrent.futures` built-in module, may be exactly what you need. It enables Python to utilize multiple CPU cores in parallel by running additional interpreters as child processes. These child processes are separate from the main interpreter, so their global interpreter locks are also separate. Each child can fully utilize one CPU core. Each child has a link to the main process where it receives instructions to do computation and returns results.

For example, say you want to do something computationally intensive with Python and utilize multiple CPU cores. I'll use an implementation of finding the greatest common divisor of two numbers as a proxy for a more computationally intense algorithm, like simulating fluid dynamics with the Navier-Stokes equation.

```
def gcd(pair):
    a, b = pair
    low = min(a, b)
    for i in range(low, 0, -1):
        if a % i == 0 and b % i == 0:
            return i
```

Running this function in serial takes a linearly increasing amount of time because there is no parallelism.

```
numbers = [(1963309, 2265973), (2030677, 3814172),
           (1551645, 2229620), (2039045, 2020802)]
start = time()
results = list(map(gcd, numbers))
end = time()
print('Took %.3f seconds' % (end - start))

>>>
Took 1.170 seconds
```

Running this code on multiple Python threads will yield no speed improvement because the GIL prevents Python from using multiple

CPU cores in parallel. Here, I do the same computation as above using the concurrent.futures module with its ThreadPoolExecutor class and two worker threads (to match the number of CPU cores on my computer):

```
start = time()
pool = ThreadPoolExecutor(max_workers=2)
results = list(pool.map(gcd, numbers))
end = time()
print('Took %.3f seconds' % (end - start))

>>>
Took 1.199 seconds
```

It's even slower this time because of the overhead of starting and communicating with the pool of threads.

Now for the surprising part: By changing a single line of code, something magical happens. If I replace the ThreadPoolExecutor with the ProcessPoolExecutor from the concurrent.futures module, everything speeds up.

```
start = time()
pool = ProcessPoolExecutor(max_workers=2)  # The one change
results = list(pool.map(gcd, numbers))
end = time()
print('Took %.3f seconds' % (end - start))

>>>
Took 0.663 seconds
```

Running on my dual-core machine, it's significantly faster! How is this possible? Here's what the ProcessPoolExecutor class actually does (via the low-level constructs provided by the multiprocessing module):

1. It takes each item from the numbers input data to map.
2. It serializes it into binary data using the pickle module (see Item 44: "Make pickle Reliable with copyreg").
3. It copies the serialized data from the main interpreter process to a child interpreter process over a local socket.
4. Next, it deserializes the data back into Python objects using pickle in the child process.
5. It then imports the Python module containing the gcd function.

6. It runs the function on the input data in parallel with other child processes.
7. It serializes the result back into bytes.
8. It copies those bytes back through the socket.
9. It deserializes the bytes back into Python objects in the parent process.
10. Finally, it merges the results from multiple children into a single list to return.

Although it looks simple to the programmer, the `multiprocessing` module and `ProcessPoolExecutor` class do a huge amount of work to make parallelism possible. In most other languages, the only touch point you need to coordinate two threads is a single lock or atomic operation. The overhead of using `multiprocessing` is high because of all of the serialization and deserialization that must happen between the parent and child processes.

This scheme is well suited to certain types of isolated, high-leverage tasks. By isolated, I mean functions that don't need to share state with other parts of the program. By high-leverage, I mean situations in which only a small amount of data must be transferred between the parent and child processes to enable a large amount of computation. The greatest common denominator algorithm is one example of this, but many other mathematical algorithms work similarly.

If your computation doesn't have these characteristics, then the overhead of `multiprocessing` may prevent it from speeding up your program through parallelization. When that happens, `multiprocessing` provides more advanced facilities for shared memory, cross-process locks, queues, and proxies. But all of these features are very complex. It's hard enough to reason about such tools in the memory space of a single process shared between Python threads. Extending that complexity to other processes and involving sockets makes this much more difficult to understand.

I suggest avoiding all parts of `multiprocessing` and using these features via the simpler `concurrent.futures` module. You can start by using the `ThreadPoolExecutor` class to run isolated, high-leverage functions in threads. Later, you can move to the `ProcessPoolExecutor` to get a speedup. Finally, once you've completely exhausted the other options, you can consider using the `multiprocessing` module directly.

### Things to Remember

- ✦ Moving CPU bottlenecks to C-extension modules can be an effective way to improve performance while maximizing your investment in Python code. However, the cost of doing so is high and may introduce bugs.
- ✦ The `multiprocessing` module provides powerful tools that can parallelize certain types of Python computation with minimal effort.
- ✦ The power of `multiprocessing` is best accessed through the `concurrent.futures` built-in module and its simple `ProcessPoolExecutor` class.
- ✦ The advanced parts of the `multiprocessing` module should be avoided because they are so complex.

# 6 Built-in Modules

Python takes a "batteries included" approach to the standard library. Many other languages ship with a small number of common packages and require you to look elsewhere for important functionality. Although Python also has an impressive repository of community-built modules, it strives to provide, in its default installation, the most important modules for common uses of the language.

The full set of standard modules is too large to cover in this book. But some of these built-in packages are so closely intertwined with idiomatic Python that they may as well be part of the language specification. These essential built-in modules are especially important when writing the intricate, error-prone parts of programs.

## Item 42: Define Function Decorators with `functools.wraps`

Python has special syntax for *decorators* that can be applied to functions. Decorators have the ability to run additional code before and after any calls to the functions they wrap. This allows them to access and modify input arguments and return values. This functionality can be useful for enforcing semantics, debugging, registering functions, and more.

For example, say you want to print the arguments and return value of a function call. This is especially helpful when debugging a stack of function calls from a recursive function. Here, I define such a decorator:

```
def trace(func):
    def wrapper(*args, **kwargs):
        result = func(*args, **kwargs)
        print('%s(%r, %r) -> %r' %
              (func.__name__, args, kwargs, result))
        return result
    return wrapper
```

I can apply this to a function using the @ symbol.

```
@trace
def fibonacci(n):
    """Return the n-th Fibonacci number"""
    if n in (0, 1):
        return n
    return (fibonacci(n - 2) + fibonacci(n - 1))
```

The @ symbol is equivalent to calling the decorator on the function it wraps and assigning the return value to the original name in the same scope.

```
fibonacci = trace(fibonacci)
```

Calling this decorated function will run the `wrapper` code before and after `fibonacci` runs, printing the arguments and return value at each level in the recursive stack.

```
fibonacci(3)

>>>
fibonacci((1,), {}) -> 1
fibonacci((0,), {}) -> 0
fibonacci((1,), {}) -> 1
fibonacci((2,), {}) -> 1
fibonacci((3,), {}) -> 2
```

This works well, but it has an unintended side effect. The value returned by the decorator—the function that's called above—doesn't think it's named `fibonacci`.

```
print(fibonacci)
>>>
<function trace.<locals>.wrapper at 0x107f7ed08>
```

The cause of this isn't hard to see. The `trace` function returns the `wrapper` it defines. The `wrapper` function is what's assigned to the `fibonacci` name in the containing module because of the decorator. This behavior is problematic because it undermines tools that do introspection, such as debuggers (see Item 57: "Consider Interactive Debugging with `pdb`") and object serializers (see Item 44: "Make `pickle` Reliable with `copyreg`").

For example, the `help` built-in function is useless on the decorated `fibonacci` function.

```
help(fibonacci)
>>>
Help on function wrapper in module __main__:

wrapper(*args, **kwargs)
```

The solution is to use the wraps helper function from the functools built-in module. This is a decorator that helps you write decorators. Applying it to the wrapper function will copy all of the important metadata about the inner function to the outer function.

```
def trace(func):
    @wraps(func)
    def wrapper(*args, **kwargs):
        # ...
    return wrapper


@trace
def fibonacci(n):
    # ...
```

Now, running the help function produces the expected result, even though the function is decorated.

```
help(fibonacci)
>>>
Help on function fibonacci in module __main__:

fibonacci(n)
    Return the n-th Fibonacci number
```

Calling help is just one example of how decorators can subtly cause problems. Python functions have many other standard attributes (e.g., `__name__`, `__module__`) that must be preserved to maintain the interface of functions in the language. Using wraps ensures that you'll always get the correct behavior.

### Things to Remember

- ✦ Decorators are Python syntax for allowing one function to modify another function at runtime.
- ✦ Using decorators can cause strange behaviors in tools that do introspection, such as debuggers.
- ✦ Use the wraps decorator from the functools built-in module when you define your own decorators to avoid any issues.

## Item 43: Consider contextlib and with Statements for Reusable try/finally Behavior

The with statement in Python is used to indicate when code is running in a special context. For example, mutual exclusion locks (see Item 38: "Use Lock to Prevent Data Races in Threads") can be used in with statements to indicate that the indented code only runs while the lock is held.

```
lock = Lock()
with lock:
    print('Lock is held')
```

The example above is equivalent to this try/finally construction because the Lock class properly enables the with statement.

```
lock.acquire()
try:
    print('Lock is held')
finally:
    lock.release()
```

The with statement version of this is better because it eliminates the need to write the repetitive code of the try/finally construction. It's easy to make your objects and functions capable of use in with statements by using the contextlib built-in module. This module contains the contextmanager decorator, which lets a simple function be used in with statements. This is much easier than defining a new class with the special methods __enter__ and __exit__ (the standard way).

For example, say you want a region of your code to have more debug logging sometimes. Here, I define a function that does logging at two severity levels:

```
def my_function():
    logging.debug('Some debug data')
    logging.error('Error log here')
    logging.debug('More debug data')
```

The default log level for my program is WARNING, so only the error message will print to screen when I run the function.

```
my_function()
>>>
Error log here
```

I can elevate the log level of this function temporarily by defining a context manager. This helper function boosts the logging severity level before running the code in the with block and reduces the logging severity level afterward.

```
@contextmanager
def debug_logging(level):
    logger = logging.getLogger()
    old_level = logger.getEffectiveLevel()
    logger.setLevel(level)
```

```
    try:
        yield
    finally:
        logger.setLevel(old_level)
```

The yield expression is the point at which the with block's contents will execute. Any exceptions that happen in the with block will be re-raised by the yield expression for you to catch in the helper function (see Item 40: "Consider Coroutines to Run Many Functions Concurrently" for an explanation of how that works).

Now, I can call the same logging function again, but in the debug_logging context. This time, all of the debug messages are printed to the screen during the with block. The same function running outside the with block won't print debug messages.

```
with debug_logging(logging.DEBUG):
    print('Inside:')
    my_function()
print('After:')
my_function()

>>>
Inside:
Some debug data
Error log here
More debug data
After:
Error log here
```

### Using with Targets

The context manager passed to a with statement may also return an object. This object is assigned to a local variable in the as part of the compound statement. This gives the code running in the with block the ability to directly interact with its context.

For example, say you want to write a file and ensure that it's always closed correctly. You can do this by passing open to the with statement. open returns a file handle for the as target of with and will close the handle when the with block exits.

```
with open('/tmp/my_output.txt', 'w') as handle:
    handle.write('This is some data!')
```

This approach is preferable to manually opening and closing the file handle every time. It gives you confidence that the file is eventually closed when execution leaves the with statement. It also encourages you to reduce the amount of code that executes while the file handle is open, which is good practice in general.

To enable your own functions to supply values for as targets, all you need to do is yield a value from your context manager. For example, here I define a context manager to fetch a Logger instance, set its level, and then yield it for the as target.

```
@contextmanager
def log_level(level, name):
    logger = logging.getLogger(name)
    old_level = logger.getEffectiveLevel()
    logger.setLevel(level)
    try:
        yield logger
    finally:
        logger.setLevel(old_level)
```

Calling logging methods like debug on the as target will produce output because the logging severity level is set low enough in the with block. Using the logging module directly won't print anything because the default logging severity level for the default program logger is WARNING.

```
with log_level(logging.DEBUG, 'my-log') as logger:
    logger.debug('This is my message!')
    logging.debug('This will not print')

>>>
This is my message!
```

After the with statement exits, calling debug logging methods on the Logger named 'my-log' will not print anything because the default logging severity level has been restored. Error log messages will always print.

```
logger = logging.getLogger('my-log')
logger.debug('Debug will not print')
logger.error('Error will print')

>>>
Error will print
```

### Things to Remember

- ✦ The with statement allows you to reuse logic from try/finally blocks and reduce visual noise.
- ✦ The contextlib built-in module provides a contextmanager decorator that makes it easy to use your own functions in with statements.
- ✦ The value yielded by context managers is supplied to the as part of the with statement. It's useful for letting your code directly access the cause of the special context.

## Item 44: Make pickle Reliable with copyreg

The pickle built-in module can serialize Python objects into a stream of bytes and deserialize bytes back into objects. Pickled byte streams shouldn't be used to communicate between untrusted parties. The purpose of pickle is to let you pass Python objects between programs that you control over binary channels.

> **Note**
>
> The pickle module's serialization format is unsafe by design. The serialized data contains what is essentially a program that describes how to reconstruct the original Python object. This means a malicious pickle payload could be used to compromise any part of the Python program that attempts to deserialize it.
>
> In contrast, the json module is safe by design. Serialized JSON data contains a simple description of an object hierarchy. Deserializing JSON data does not expose a Python program to any additional risk. Formats like JSON should be used for communication between programs or people that don't trust each other.

For example, say you want to use a Python object to represent the state of a player's progress in a game. The game state includes the level the player is on and the number of lives he or she has remaining.

```
class GameState(object):
    def __init__(self):
        self.level = 0
        self.lives = 4
```

The program modifies this object as the game runs.

```
state = GameState()
state.level += 1  # Player beat a level
state.lives -= 1  # Player had to try again
```

When the user quits playing, the program can save the state of the game to a file so it can be resumed at a later time. The pickle module makes it easy to do this. Here, I dump the GameState object directly to a file:

```
state_path = '/tmp/game_state.bin'
with open(state_path, 'wb') as f:
    pickle.dump(state, f)
```

Later, I can load the file and get back the GameState object as if it had never been serialized.

```
with open(state_path, 'rb') as f:
    state_after = pickle.load(f)
print(state_after.__dict__)
```

```
>>>
{'lives': 3, 'level': 1}
```

The problem with this approach is what happens as the game's features expand over time. Imagine you want the player to earn points towards a high score. To track the player's points, you'd add a new field to the GameState class.

```
class GameState(object):
    def __init__(self):
        # ...
        self.points = 0
```

Serializing the new version of the GameState class using pickle will work exactly as before. Here, I simulate the round-trip through a file by serializing to a string with dumps and back to an object with loads:

```
state = GameState()
serialized = pickle.dumps(state)
state_after = pickle.loads(serialized)
print(state_after.__dict__)

>>>
{'lives': 4, 'level': 0, 'points': 0}
```

But what happens to older saved GameState objects that the user may want to resume? Here, I unpickle an old game file using a program with the new definition of the GameState class:

```
with open(state_path, 'rb') as f:
    state_after = pickle.load(f)
print(state_after.__dict__)

>>>
{'lives': 3, 'level': 1}
```

The points attribute is missing! This is especially confusing because the returned object is an instance of the new GameState class.

```
assert isinstance(state_after, GameState)
```

This behavior is a byproduct of the way the pickle module works. Its primary use case is making it easy to serialize objects. As soon as your use of pickle expands beyond trivial usage, the module's functionality starts to break down in surprising ways.

Fixing these problems is straightforward using the copyreg built-in module. The copyreg module lets you register the functions responsible for serializing Python objects, allowing you to control the behavior of pickle and make it more reliable.

### Default Attribute Values

In the simplest case, you can use a constructor with default arguments (see Item 19: "Provide Optional Behavior with Keyword Arguments") to ensure that GameState objects will always have all attributes after unpickling. Here, I redefine the constructor this way:

```
class GameState(object):
    def __init__(self, level=0, lives=4, points=0):
        self.level = level
        self.lives = lives
        self.points = points
```

To use this constructor for pickling, I define a helper function that takes a GameState object and turns it into a tuple of parameters for the copyreg module. The returned tuple contains the function to use for unpickling and the parameters to pass to the unpickling function.

```
def pickle_game_state(game_state):
    kwargs = game_state.__dict__
    return unpickle_game_state, (kwargs,)
```

Now, I need to define the unpickle_game_state helper. This function takes serialized data and parameters from pickle_game_state and returns the corresponding GameState object. It's a tiny wrapper around the constructor.

```
def unpickle_game_state(kwargs):
    return GameState(**kwargs)
```

Now, I register these with the copyreg built-in module.

```
copyreg.pickle(GameState, pickle_game_state)
```

Serializing and deserializing works as before.

```
state = GameState()
state.points += 1000
serialized = pickle.dumps(state)
state_after = pickle.loads(serialized)
print(state_after.__dict__)

>>>
{'lives': 4, 'level': 0, 'points': 1000}
```

With this registration done, now I can change the definition of GameState to give the player a count of magic spells to use. This change is similar to when I added the points field to GameState.

```
class GameState(object):
    def __init__(self, level=0, lives=4, points=0, magic=5):
        # ...
```

But unlike before, deserializing an old GameState object will result in valid game data instead of missing attributes. This works because unpickle_game_state calls the GameState constructor directly. The constructor's keyword arguments have default values when parameters are missing. This causes old game state files to receive the default value for the new magic field when they are deserialized.

```
state_after = pickle.loads(serialized)
print(state_after.__dict__)

>>>
{'level': 0, 'points': 1000, 'magic': 5, 'lives': 4}
```

### Versioning Classes

Sometimes you'll need to make backwards-incompatible changes to your Python objects by removing fields. This prevents the default argument approach to serialization from working.

For example, say you realize that a limited number of lives is a bad idea, and you want to remove the concept of lives from the game. Here, I redefine the GameState to no longer have a lives field:

```
class GameState(object):
    def __init__(self, level=0, points=0, magic=5):
        # ...
```

The problem is that this breaks deserializing old game data. All fields from the old data, even ones removed from the class, will be passed to the GameState constructor by the unpickle_game_state function.

```
pickle.loads(serialized)

>>>
TypeError: __init__() got an unexpected keyword argument
➥'lives'
```

The solution is to add a version parameter to the functions supplied to copyreg. New serialized data will have a version of 2 specified when pickling a new GameState object.

```
def pickle_game_state(game_state):
    kwargs = game_state.__dict__
    kwargs['version'] = 2
    return unpickle_game_state, (kwargs,)
```

Old versions of the data will not have a version argument present, allowing you to manipulate the arguments passed to the GameState constructor accordingly.

```
def unpickle_game_state(kwargs):
    version = kwargs.pop('version', 1)
    if version == 1:
        kwargs.pop('lives')
    return GameState(**kwargs)
```

Now, deserializing an old object works properly.

```
copyreg.pickle(GameState, pickle_game_state)
state_after = pickle.loads(serialized)
print(state_after.__dict__)

>>>
{'magic': 5, 'level': 0, 'points': 1000}
```

You can continue this approach to handle changes between future versions of the same class. Any logic you need to adapt an old version of the class to a new version of the class can go in the unpickle_game_state function.

**Stable Import Paths**

One other issue you may encounter with pickle is breakage from renaming a class. Often over the life cycle of a program, you'll refactor your code by renaming classes and moving them to other modules. Unfortunately, this will break the pickle module unless you're careful.

Here, I rename the GameState class to BetterGameState, removing the old class from the program entirely:

```
class BetterGameState(object):
    def __init__(self, level=0, points=0, magic=5):
        # ...
```

Attempting to deserialize an old GameState object will now fail because the class can't be found.

```
pickle.loads(serialized)
>>>
AttributeError: Can't get attribute 'GameState' on <module
➥'__main__' from 'my_code.py'>
```

The cause of this exception is that the import path of the serialized object's class is encoded in the pickled data.

```
print(serialized[:25])
>>>
b'\x80\x03c__main__\nGameState\nq\x00)'
```

The solution is to use copyreg again. You can specify a stable identifier for the function to use for unpickling an object. This allows you to transition pickled data to different classes with different names when it's deserialized. It gives you a level of indirection.

```
copyreg.pickle(BetterGameState, pickle_game_state)
```

After using copyreg, you can see that the import path to pickle_game_state is encoded in the serialized data instead of BetterGameState.

```
state = BetterGameState()
serialized = pickle.dumps(state)
print(serialized[:35])

>>>
b'\x80\x03c__main__\nunpickle_game_state\nq\x00}'
```

The only gotcha is that you can't change the path of the module in which the unpickle_game_state function is present. Once you serialize data with a function, it must remain available on that import path for deserializing in the future.

### Things to Remember

- The pickle built-in module is only useful for serializing and deserializing objects between trusted programs.
- The pickle module may break down when used for more than trivial use cases.
- Use the copyreg built-in module with pickle to add missing attribute values, allow versioning of classes, and provide stable import paths.

## Item 45: Use datetime Instead of time for Local Clocks

Coordinated Universal Time (UTC) is the standard, time-zone-independent representation of time. UTC works great for computers that represent time as seconds since the UNIX epoch. But UTC isn't ideal for humans. Humans reference time relative to where they're currently located. People say "noon" or "8 am" instead of "UTC 15:00 minus 7 hours." If your program handles time, you'll probably find yourself converting time between UTC and local clocks to make it easier for humans to understand.

Python provides two ways of accomplishing time zone conversions. The old way, using the time built-in module, is disastrously error prone. The new way, using the datetime built-in module, works great with some help from the community-built package named pytz.

You should be acquainted with both time and datetime to thoroughly understand why datetime is the best choice and time should be avoided.

### The time Module

The localtime function from the time built-in module lets you convert a UNIX timestamp (seconds since the UNIX epoch in UTC) to a local time that matches the host computer's time zone (Pacific Daylight Time, in my case).

```
from time import localtime, strftime

now = 1407694710
local_tuple = localtime(now)
time_format = '%Y-%m-%d %H:%M:%S'
time_str = strftime(time_format, local_tuple)
print(time_str)

>>>
2014-08-10 11:18:30
```

You'll often need to go the other way as well, starting with user input in local time and converting it to UTC time. You can do this by using the strptime function to parse the time string, then call mktime to convert local time to a UNIX timestamp.

```
from time import mktime, strptime

time_tuple = strptime(time_str, time_format)
utc_now = mktime(time_tuple)
print(utc_now)

>>>
1407694710.0
```

How do you convert local time in one time zone to local time in another? For example, say you are taking a flight between San Francisco and New York, and want to know what time it will be in San Francisco once you've arrived in New York.

Directly manipulating the return values from the time, localtime, and strptime functions to do time zone conversions is a bad idea. Time zones change all the time due to local laws. It's too complicated to manage yourself, especially if you want to handle every global city for flight departure and arrival.

Many operating systems have configuration files that keep up with the time zone changes automatically. Python lets you use these time zones through the `time` module. For example, here I parse the departure time from the San Francisco time zone of Pacific Daylight Time:

```
parse_format = '%Y-%m-%d %H:%M:%S %Z'
depart_sfo = '2014-05-01 15:45:16 PDT'
time_tuple = strptime(depart_sfo, parse_format)
time_str = strftime(time_format, time_tuple)
print(time_str)

>>>
2014-05-01 15:45:16
```

After seeing that PDT works with the `strptime` function, you might also assume that other time zones known to my computer will also work. Unfortunately, this isn't the case. Instead, `strptime` raises an exception when it sees Eastern Daylight Time (the time zone for New York).

```
arrival_nyc = '2014-05-01 23:33:24 EDT'
time_tuple = strptime(arrival_nyc, time_format)

>>>
ValueError: unconverted data remains:  EDT
```

The problem here is the platform-dependent nature of the `time` module. Its actual behavior is determined by how the underlying C functions work with the host operating system. This makes the functionality of the `time` module unreliable in Python. The `time` module fails to consistently work properly for multiple local times. Thus, you should avoid the `time` module for this purpose. If you must use `time`, only use it to convert between UTC and the host computer's local time. For all other types of conversions, use the `datetime` module.

### The datetime Module

The second option for representing times in Python is the `datetime` class from the `datetime` built-in module. Like the `time` module, `datetime` can be used to convert from the current time in UTC to local time.

Here, I take the present time in UTC and convert it to my computer's local time (Pacific Daylight Time):

```
from datetime import datetime, timezone


now = datetime(2014, 8, 10, 18, 18, 30)
now_utc = now.replace(tzinfo=timezone.utc)
now_local = now_utc.astimezone()
print(now_local)

>>>
2014-08-10 11:18:30-07:00
```

The datetime module can also easily convert a local time back to a UNIX timestamp in UTC.

```
time_str = '2014-08-10 11:18:30'
now = datetime.strptime(time_str, time_format)
time_tuple = now.timetuple()
utc_now = mktime(time_tuple)
print(utc_now)

>>>
1407694710.0
```

Unlike the time module, the datetime module has facilities for reliably converting from one local time to another local time. However, datetime only provides the machinery for time zone operations with its tzinfo class and related methods. What's missing are the time zone definitions besides UTC.

Luckily, the Python community has addressed this gap with the pytz module that's available for download from the Python Package Index (https://pypi.python.org/pypi/pytz/). pytz contains a full database of every time zone definition you might need.

To use pytz effectively, you should always convert local times to UTC first. Perform any datetime operations you need on the UTC values (such as offsetting). Then, convert to local times as a final step.

For example, here I convert an NYC flight arrival time to a UTC datetime. Although some of these calls seem redundant, all of them are necessary when using pytz.

```
arrival_nyc = '2014-05-01 23:33:24'
nyc_dt_naive = datetime.strptime(arrival_nyc, time_format)
eastern = pytz.timezone('US/Eastern')
nyc_dt = eastern.localize(nyc_dt_naive)
utc_dt = pytz.utc.normalize(nyc_dt.astimezone(pytz.utc))
print(utc_dt)

>>>
2014-05-02 03:33:24+00:00
```

Once I have a UTC datetime, I can convert it to San Francisco local time.

```
pacific = pytz.timezone('US/Pacific')
sf_dt = pacific.normalize(utc_dt.astimezone(pacific))
print(sf_dt)

>>>
2014-05-01 20:33:24-07:00
```

Just as easily, I can convert it to the local time in Nepal.

```
nepal = pytz.timezone('Asia/Katmandu')
nepal_dt = nepal.normalize(utc_dt.astimezone(nepal))
print(nepal_dt)

>>>
2014-05-02 09:18:24+05:45
```

With `datetime` and `pytz`, these conversions are consistent across all environments regardless of what operating system the host computer is running.

### Things to Remember

- ✦ Avoid using the `time` module for translating between different time zones.
- ✦ Use the `datetime` built-in module along with the `pytz` module to reliably convert between times in different time zones.
- ✦ Always represent time in UTC and do conversions to local time as the final step before presentation.

## Item 46: Use Built-in Algorithms and Data Structures

When you're implementing Python programs that handle a non-trivial amount of data, you'll eventually see slowdowns caused by the algorithmic complexity of your code. This usually isn't the result of Python's speed as a language (see Item 41: "Consider `concurrent.futures` for True Parallelism" if it is). The issue, more likely, is that you aren't using the best algorithms and data structures for your problem.

Luckily, the Python standard library has many of the algorithms and data structures you'll need to use built in. Besides speed, using these common algorithms and data structures can make your life easier. Some of the most valuable tools you may want to use are tricky to implement correctly. Avoiding reimplementation of common functionality will save you time and headaches.

### Double-ended Queue

The `deque` class from the `collections` module is a double-ended queue. It provides constant time operations for inserting or removing items from its beginning or end. This makes it ideal for first-in-first-out (FIFO) queues.

```
fifo = deque()
fifo.append(1)      # Producer
x = fifo.popleft()  # Consumer
```

The `list` built-in type also contains an ordered sequence of items like a queue. You can insert or remove items from the end of a list in constant time. But inserting or removing items from the head of a list takes linear time, which is much slower than the constant time of a `deque`.

### Ordered Dictionary

Standard dictionaries are unordered. That means a `dict` with the same keys and values can result in different orders of iteration. This behavior is a surprising byproduct of the way the dictionary's fast hash table is implemented.

```
a = {}
a['foo'] = 1
a['bar'] = 2

# Randomly populate 'b' to cause hash conflicts
while True:
    z = randint(99, 1013)
    b = {}
    for i in range(z):
        b[i] = i
    b['foo'] = 1
    b['bar'] = 2
    for i in range(z):
        del b[i]
    if str(b) != str(a):
        break

print(a)
print(b)
print('Equal?', a == b)

>>>
{'foo': 1, 'bar': 2}
{'bar': 2, 'foo': 1}
Equal? True
```

The `OrderedDict` class from the `collections` module is a special type of dictionary that keeps track of the order in which its keys were inserted. Iterating the keys of an `OrderedDict` has predictable behavior. This can vastly simplify testing and debugging by making all code deterministic.

```
a = OrderedDict()
a['foo'] = 1
a['bar'] = 2
```

```
b = OrderedDict()
b['foo'] = 'red'
b['bar'] = 'blue'

for value1, value2 in zip(a.values(), b.values()):
    print(value1, value2)

>>>
1 red
2 blue
```

### Default Dictionary

Dictionaries are useful for bookkeeping and tracking statistics. One problem with dictionaries is that you can't assume any keys are already present. That makes it clumsy to do simple things like increment a counter stored in a dictionary.

```
stats = {}
key = 'my_counter'
if key not in stats:
    stats[key] = 0
stats[key] += 1
```

The `defaultdict` class from the `collections` module simplifies this by automatically storing a default value when a key doesn't exist. All you have to do is provide a function that will return the default value each time a key is missing. In this example, the `int` built-in function returns `0` (see Item 23: "Accept Functions for Simple Interfaces Instead of Classes" for another example). Now, incrementing a counter is simple.

```
stats = defaultdict(int)
stats['my_counter'] += 1
```

### Heap Queue

Heaps are useful data structures for maintaining a priority queue. The `heapq` module provides functions for creating heaps in standard `list` types with functions like `heappush`, `heappop`, and `nsmallest`.

Items of any priority can be inserted into the heap in any order.

```
a = []
heappush(a, 5)
heappush(a, 3)
heappush(a, 7)
heappush(a, 4)
```

Items are always removed by highest priority (lowest number) first.

```
print(heappop(a), heappop(a), heappop(a), heappop(a))
>>>
3 4 5 7
```

The resulting `list` is easy to use outside of `heapq`. Accessing the `0` index of the heap will always return the smallest item.

```
a = []
heappush(a, 5)
heappush(a, 3)
heappush(a, 7)
heappush(a, 4)
assert a[0] == nsmallest(1, a)[0] == 3
```

Calling the `sort` method on the `list` maintains the heap invariant.

```
print('Before:', a)
a.sort()
print('After: ', a)

>>>
Before: [3, 4, 7, 5]
After:  [3, 4, 5, 7]
```

Each of these `heapq` operations takes logarithmic time in proportion to the length of the list. Doing the same work with a standard Python list would scale linearly.

## Bisection

Searching for an item in a `list` takes linear time proportional to its length when you call the `index` method.

```
x = list(range(10**6))
i = x.index(991234)
```

The `bisect` module's functions, such as `bisect_left`, provide an efficient binary search through a sequence of sorted items. The index it returns is the insertion point of the value into the sequence.

```
i = bisect_left(x, 991234)
```

The complexity of a binary search is logarithmic. That means using `bisect` to search a list of 1 million items takes roughly the same amount of time as using `index` to linearly search a list of 14 items. It's way faster!

## Iterator Tools

The `itertools` built-in module contains a large number of functions that are useful for organizing and interacting with iterators (see

Item 16: "Consider Generators Instead of Returning Lists" and Item 17: "Be Defensive When Iterating Over Arguments" for background). Not all of these are available in Python 2, but they can easily be built using simple recipes documented in the module. See `help(itertools)` in an interactive Python session for more details.

The `itertools` functions fall into three main categories:

- Linking iterators together
  - `chain`: Combines multiple iterators into a single sequential iterator.
  - `cycle`: Repeats an iterator's items forever.
  - `tee`: Splits a single iterator into multiple parallel iterators.
  - `zip_longest`: A variant of the `zip` built-in function that works well with iterators of different lengths.
- Filtering items from an iterator
  - `islice`: Slices an iterator by numerical indexes without copying.
  - `takewhile`: Returns items from an iterator while a predicate function returns `True`.
  - `dropwhile`: Returns items from an iterator once the predicate function returns `False` for the first time.
  - `filterfalse`: Returns all items from an iterator where a predicate function returns `False`. The opposite of the `filter` built-in function.
- Combinations of items from iterators
  - `product`: Returns the Cartesian product of items from an iterator, which is a nice alternative to deeply nested list comprehensions.
  - `permutations`: Returns ordered permutations of length N with items from an iterator.
  - `combination`: Returns the unordered combinations of length N with unrepeated items from an iterator.

There are even more functions and recipes available in the `itertools` module that I don't mention here. Whenever you find yourself dealing with some tricky iteration code, it's worth looking at the `itertools` documentation again to see whether there's anything there for you to use.

### Things to Remember

✦ Use Python's built-in modules for algorithms and data structures.

✦ Don't reimplement this functionality yourself. It's hard to get right.

## Item 47: Use decimal When Precision Is Paramount

Python is an excellent language for writing code that interacts with numerical data. Python's integer type can represent values of any practical size. Its double-precision floating point type complies with the IEEE 754 standard. The language also provides a standard complex number type for imaginary values. However, these aren't enough for every situation.

For example, say you want to compute the amount to charge a customer for an international phone call. You know the time in minutes and seconds that the customer was on the phone (say, 3 minutes 42 seconds). You also have a set rate for the cost of calling Antarctica from the United States ($1.45/minute). What should the charge be?

With floating point math, the computed charge seems reasonable.

```
rate = 1.45
seconds = 3*60 + 42
cost = rate * seconds / 60
print(cost)

>>>
5.364999999999999
```

But rounding it to the nearest whole cent rounds down when you want it to round up to properly cover all costs incurred by the customer.

```
print(round(cost, 2))

>>>
5.36
```

Say you also want to support very short phone calls between places that are much cheaper to connect. Here, I compute the charge for a phone call that was 5 seconds long with a rate of $0.05/minute:

```
rate = 0.05
seconds = 5
cost = rate * seconds / 60
print(cost)

>>>
0.004166666666666667
```

The resulting float is so low that it rounds down to zero. This won't do!

```
print(round(cost, 2))
>>>
0.0
```

The solution is to use the Decimal class from the decimal built-in module. The Decimal class provides fixed point math of 28 decimal points by default. It can go even higher if required. This works around the precision issues in IEEE 754 floating point numbers. The class also gives you more control over rounding behaviors.

For example, redoing the Antarctica calculation with Decimal results in an exact charge instead of an approximation.

```
rate = Decimal('1.45')
seconds = Decimal('222')  # 3*60 + 42
cost = rate * seconds / Decimal('60')
print(cost)

>>>
5.365
```

The Decimal class has a built-in function for rounding to exactly the decimal place you need with the rounding behavior you want.

```
rounded = cost.quantize(Decimal('0.01'), rounding=ROUND_UP)
print(rounded)

>>>
5.37
```

Using the quantize method this way also properly handles the small usage case for short, cheap phone calls. Here, you can see the Decimal cost is still less than 1 cent for the call:

```
rate = Decimal('0.05')
seconds = Decimal('5')
cost = rate * seconds / Decimal('60')
print(cost)

>>>
0.004166666666666666666666666667
```

But the quantize behavior ensures that this is rounded up to one whole cent.

```
rounded = cost.quantize(Decimal('0.01'), rounding=ROUND_UP)
print(rounded)

>>>
0.01
```

While Decimal works great for fixed point numbers, it still has limitations in its precision (e.g., 1/3 will be an approximation). For representing rational numbers with no limit to precision, consider using the Fraction class from the fractions built-in module.

**Things to Remember**

- ✦ Python has built-in types and classes in modules that can represent practically every type of numerical value.
- ✦ The `Decimal` class is ideal for situations that require high precision and exact rounding behavior, such as computations of monetary values.

## Item 48: Know Where to Find Community-Built Modules

Python has a central repository of modules (https://pypi.python.org) for you to install and use in your programs. These modules are built and maintained by people like you: the Python community. When you find yourself facing an unfamiliar challenge, the Python Package Index (PyPI) is a great place to look for code that will get you closer to your goal.

To use the Package Index, you'll need to use a command-line tool named `pip`. `pip` is installed by default in Python 3.4 and above (it's also accessible with `python -m pip`). For earlier versions, you can find instructions for installing `pip` on the Python Packaging website (https://packaging.python.org).

Once installed, using `pip` to install a new module is simple. For example, here I install the `pytz` module that I used in another item in this chapter (see Item 45: "Use `datetime` Instead of `time` for Local Clocks"):

```
$ pip3 install pytz
Downloading/unpacking pytz
  Downloading pytz-2014.4.tar.bz2 (159kB): 159kB downloaded
  Running setup.py (...) egg_info for package pytz

Installing collected packages: pytz
  Running setup.py install for pytz

Successfully installed pytz
Cleaning up...
```

In the example above, I used the `pip3` command-line to install the Python 3 version of the package. The `pip` command-line (without the 3) is also available for installing packages for Python 2. The majority of popular packages are now available for either version of Python (see Item 1: "Know Which Version of Python You're Using"). `pip` can also be used with `pyvenv` to track sets of packages to install for your projects (see Item 53: "Use Virtual Environments for Isolated and Reproducible Dependencies").

Each module in the PyPI has its own software license. Most of the packages, especially the popular ones, have free or open source licenses (see http://opensource.org for details). In most cases, these licenses allow you to include a copy of the module with your program (when in doubt, talk to a lawyer).

### Things to Remember

- The Python Package Index (PyPI) contains a wealth of common packages that are built and maintained by the Python community.
- `pip` is the command-line tool to use for installing packages from PyPI.
- `pip` is installed by default in Python 3.4 and above; you must install it yourself for older versions.
- The majority of PyPI modules are free and open source software.

# 7 Collaboration

There are language features in Python to help you construct well-defined APIs with clear interface boundaries. The Python community has established best practices that maximize the maintainability of code over time. There are also standard tools that ship with Python that enable large teams to work together across disparate environments.

Collaborating with others on Python programs requires being deliberate about how you write your code. Even if you're working on your own, chances are you'll be using code written by someone else via the standard library or open source packages. It's important to understand the mechanisms that make it easy to collaborate with other Python programmers.

## Item 49: Write Docstrings for Every Function, Class, and Module

Documentation in Python is extremely important because of the dynamic nature of the language. Python provides built-in support for attaching documentation to blocks of code. Unlike many other languages, the documentation from a program's source code is directly accessible as the program runs.

For example, you can add documentation by providing a *docstring* immediately after the `def` statement of a function.

```
def palindrome(word):
    """Return True if the given word is a palindrome."""
    return word == word[::-1]
```

You can retrieve the docstring from within the Python program itself by accessing the function's `__doc__` special attribute.

```
print(repr(palindrome.__doc__))
```

```
>>>
'Return True if the given word is a palindrome.'
```

Docstrings can be attached to functions, classes, and modules. This connection is part of the process of compiling and running a Python program. Support for docstrings and the `__doc__` attribute has three consequences:

- The accessibility of documentation makes interactive development easier. You can inspect functions, classes, and modules to see their documentation by using the `help` built-in function. This makes the Python interactive interpreter (the Python "shell") and tools like IPython Notebook (http://ipython.org) a joy to use while you're developing algorithms, testing APIs, and writing code snippets.
- A standard way of defining documentation makes it easy to build tools that convert the text into more appealing formats (like HTML). This has led to excellent documentation-generation tools for the Python community, such as Sphinx (http://sphinx-doc.org). It's also enabled community-funded sites like Read the Docs (https://readthedocs.org) that provide free hosting of beautiful-looking documentation for open source Python projects.
- Python's first-class, accessible, and good-looking documentation encourages people to write more documentation. The members of the Python community have a strong belief in the importance of documentation. There's an assumption that "good code" also means well-documented code. This means that you can expect most open source Python libraries to have decent documentation.

To participate in this excellent culture of documentation, you need to follow a few guidelines when you write docstrings. The full details are discussed online in PEP 257 (http://www.python.org/dev/peps/pep-0257/). There are a few best-practices you should be sure to follow.

### Documenting Modules

Each module should have a top-level docstring. This is a string literal that is the first statement in a source file. It should use three double quotes ("""). The goal of this docstring is to introduce the module and its contents.

The first line of the docstring should be a single sentence describing the module's purpose. The paragraphs that follow should contain the details that all users of the module should know about its operation. The module docstring is also a jumping-off point where you can highlight important classes and functions found in the module.

Here's an example of a module docstring:

```
# words.py
#!/usr/bin/env python3
"""Library for testing words for various linguistic patterns.

Testing how words relate to each other can be tricky sometimes!
This module provides easy ways to determine when words you've
found have special properties.

Available functions:
- palindrome: Determine if a word is a palindrome.
- check_anagram: Determine if two words are anagrams.
...
"""

# ...
```

If the module is a command-line utility, the module docstring is also a great place to put usage information for running the tool from the command-line.

### Documenting Classes

Each class should have a class-level docstring. This largely follows the same pattern as the module-level docstring. The first line is the single-sentence purpose of the class. Paragraphs that follow discuss important details of the class's operation.

Important public attributes and methods of the class should be highlighted in the class-level docstring. It should also provide guidance to subclasses on how to properly interact with protected attributes (see Item 27: "Prefer Public Attributes Over Private Ones") and the superclass's methods.

Here's an example of a class docstring:

```
class Player(object):
    """Represents a player of the game.

    Subclasses may override the 'tick' method to provide
    custom animations for the player's movement depending
    on their power level, etc.

    Public attributes:
    - power: Unused power-ups (float between 0 and 1).
    - coins: Coins found during the level (integer).
    """

    # ...
```

### Documenting Functions

Each public function and method should have a docstring. This follows the same pattern as modules and classes. The first line is the single-sentence description of what the function does. The paragraphs that follow should describe any specific behaviors and the arguments for the function. Any return values should be mentioned. Any exceptions that callers must handle as part of the function's interface should be explained.

Here's an example of a function docstring:

```
def find_anagrams(word, dictionary):
    """Find all anagrams for a word.

    This function only runs as fast as the test for
    membership in the 'dictionary' container. It will
    be slow if the dictionary is a list and fast if
    it's a set.

    Args:
        word: String of the target word.
        dictionary: Container with all strings that
            are known to be actual words.

    Returns:
        List of anagrams that were found. Empty if
        none were found.
    """
    # ...
```

There are also some special cases in writing docstrings for functions that are important to know.

- If your function has no arguments and a simple return value, a single sentence description is probably good enough.
- If your function doesn't return anything, it's better to leave out any mention of the return value instead of saying "returns None."
- If you don't expect your function to raise an exception during normal operation, don't mention that fact.
- If your function accepts a variable number of arguments (see Item 18: "Reduce Visual Noise with Variable Positional Arguments") or keyword-arguments (see Item 19: "Provide Optional Behavior with Keyword Arguments"), use `*args` and `**kwargs` in the documented list of arguments to describe their purpose.

- If your function has arguments with default values, those defaults should be mentioned (see Item 20: "Use None and Docstrings to Specify Dynamic Default Arguments").
- If your function is a generator (see Item 16: "Consider Generators Instead of Returning Lists"), then your docstring should describe what the generator yields when it's iterated.
- If your function is a coroutine (see Item 40: "Consider Coroutines to Run Many Functions Concurrently"), then your docstring should contain what the coroutine yields, what it expects to receive from `yield` expressions, and when it will stop iteration.

Note

Once you've written docstrings for your modules, it's important to keep the documentation up to date. The `doctest` built-in module makes it easy to exercise usage examples embedded in docstrings to ensure that your source code and its documentation don't diverge over time.

### Things to Remember

- ✦ Write documentation for every module, class, and function using docstrings. Keep them up to date as your code changes.
- ✦ For modules: Introduce the contents of the module and any important classes or functions all users should know about.
- ✦ For classes: Document behavior, important attributes, and subclass behavior in the docstring following the `class` statement.
- ✦ For functions and methods: Document every argument, returned value, raised exception, and other behaviors in the docstring following the `def` statement.

## Item 50: Use Packages to Organize Modules and Provide Stable APIs

As the size of a program's codebase grows, it's natural for you to reorganize its structure. You split larger functions into smaller functions. You refactor data structures into helper classes (see Item 22: "Prefer Helper Classes Over Bookkeeping with Dictionaries and Tuples"). You separate functionality into various modules that depend on each other.

At some point, you'll find yourself with so many modules that you need another layer in your program to make it understandable. For this purpose, Python provides *packages*. Packages are modules that contain other modules.

In most cases, packages are defined by putting an empty file named `__init__.py` into a directory. Once `__init__.py` is present, any other Python files in that directory will be available for import using a path relative to the directory. For example, imagine that you have the following directory structure in your program.

```
main.py
mypackage/__init__.py
mypackage/models.py
mypackage/utils.py
```

To import the `utils` module, you use the absolute module name that includes the package directory's name.

```
# main.py
from mypackage import utils
```

This pattern continues when you have package directories present within other packages (like `mypackage.foo.bar`).

> Note
>
> Python 3.4 introduces *namespace packages*, a more flexible way to define packages. Namespace packages can be composed of modules from completely separate directories, zip archives, or even remote systems. For details on how to use the advanced features of namespace packages, see PEP 420 (http://www.python.org/dev/peps/pep-0420/).

The functionality provided by packages has two primary purposes in Python programs.

### Namespaces

The first use of packages is to help divide your modules into separate namespaces. This allows you to have many modules with the same filename but different absolute paths that are unique. For example, here's a program that imports attributes from two modules with the same name, `utils.py`. This works because the modules can be addressed by their absolute paths.

```
# main.py
from analysis.utils import log_base2_bucket
from frontend.utils import stringify

bucket = stringify(log_base2_bucket(33))
```

This approach breaks down when the functions, classes, or submodules defined in packages have the same names. For example, say you want to use the `inspect` function from both the `analysis.utils` and frontend.utils modules. Importing the attributes directly won't work because the second import statement will overwrite the value of inspect in the current scope.

```
# main2.py
from analysis.utils import inspect
from frontend.utils import inspect  # Overwrites!
```

The solution is to use the as clause of the import statement to rename whatever you've imported for the current scope.

```
# main3.py
from analysis.utils import inspect as analysis_inspect
from frontend.utils import inspect as frontend_inspect

value = 33
if analysis_inspect(value) == frontend_inspect(value):
    print('Inspection equal!')
```

The as clause can be used to rename anything you retrieve with the import statement, including entire modules. This makes it easy to access namespaced code and make its identity clear when you use it.

> **Note**
>
> Another approach for avoiding imported name conflicts is to always access names by their highest unique module name.
>
> For the example above, you'd first import analysis.utils and import frontend.utils. Then, you'd access the inspect functions with the full paths of analysis.utils.inspect and frontend.utils.inspect.
>
> This approach allows you to avoid the as clause altogether. It also makes it abundantly clear to new readers of the code where each function is defined.

### Stable APIs

The second use of packages in Python is to provide strict, stable APIs for external consumers.

When you're writing an API for wider consumption, like an open source package (see Item 48: "Know Where to Find Community-Built Modules"), you'll want to provide stable functionality that doesn't change between releases. To ensure that happens, it's important to hide your internal code organization from external users. This enables you to refactor and improve your package's internal modules without breaking existing users.

Python can limit the surface area exposed to API consumers by using the __all__ special attribute of a module or package. The value of `__all__` is a list of every name to export from the module as part of its public API. When consuming code does `from foo import *`, only the attributes in `foo.__all__` will be imported from `foo`. If `__all__` isn't present in `foo`, then only public attributes, those without a leading underscore, are imported (see Item 27: "Prefer Public Attributes Over Private Ones").

For example, say you want to provide a package for calculating collisions between moving projectiles. Here, I define the `models` module of `mypackage` to contain the representation of projectiles:

```
# models.py
__all__ = ['Projectile']

class Projectile(object):
    def __init__(self, mass, velocity):
        self.mass = mass
        self.velocity = velocity
```

I also define a `utils` module in `mypackage` to perform operations on the `Projectile` instances, such as simulating collisions between them.

```
# utils.py
from . models import Projectile

__all__ = ['simulate_collision']

def _dot_product(a, b):
    # ...

def simulate_collision(a, b):
    # ...
```

Now, I'd like to provide all of the public parts of this API as a set of attributes that are available on the `mypackage` module. This will allow downstream consumers to always import directly from `mypackage` instead of importing from `mypackage.models` or `mypackage.utils`. This ensures that the API consumer's code will continue to work even if the internal organization of `mypackage` changes (e.g., `models.py` is deleted).

To do this with Python packages, you need to modify the `__init__.py` file in the `mypackage` directory. This file actually becomes the contents of the `mypackage` module when it's imported. Thus, you can specify an explicit API for `mypackage` by limiting what you import into `__init__.py`. Since all of my internal modules already specify `__all__`, I can expose the public interface of `mypackage` by simply importing everything from the internal modules and updating `__all__` accordingly.

```
# __init__.py
__all__ = []
from . models import *
__all__ += models.__all__
from . utils import *
__all__ += utils.__all__
```

Here's a consumer of the API that directly imports from mypackage instead of accessing the inner modules:

```
# api_consumer.py
from mypackage import *

a = Projectile(1.5, 3)
b = Projectile(4, 1.7)
after_a, after_b = simulate_collision(a, b)
```

Notably, internal-only functions like `mypackage.utils._dot_product` will not be available to the API consumer on `mypackage` because they weren't present in `__all__`. Being omitted from `__all__` means they weren't imported by the `from mypackage import *` statement. The internal-only names are effectively hidden.

This whole approach works great when it's important to provide an explicit, stable API. However, if you're building an API for use between your own modules, the functionality of `__all__` is probably unnecessary and should be avoided. The namespacing provided by packages is usually enough for a team of programmers to collaborate on large amounts of code they control while maintaining reasonable interface boundaries.

### Beware of `import *`

Import statements like `from x import y` are clear because the source of `y` is explicitly the `x` package or module. Wildcard imports like `from foo import *` can also be useful, especially in interactive Python sessions. However, wildcards make code more difficult to understand.

- `from foo import *` hides the source of names from new readers of the code. If a module has multiple `import *` statements, you'll need to check all of the referenced modules to figure out where a name was defined.
- Names from `import *` statements will overwrite any conflicting names within the containing module. This can lead to strange bugs caused by accidental interactions between your code and overlapping names from multiple `import *` statements.

The safest approach is to avoid `import *` in your code and explicitly import names with the `from x import y` style.

**Things to Remember**

- ✦ Packages in Python are modules that contain other modules. Packages allow you to organize your code into separate, non-conflicting namespaces with unique absolute module names.
- ✦ Simple packages are defined by adding an `__init__.py` file to a directory that contains other source files. These files become the child modules of the directory's package. Package directories may also contain other packages.
- ✦ You can provide an explicit API for a module by listing its publicly visible names in its `__all__` special attribute.
- ✦ You can hide a package's internal implementation by only importing public names in the package's `__init__.py` file or by naming internal-only members with a leading underscore.
- ✦ When collaborating within a single team or on a single codebase, using `__all__` for explicit APIs is probably unnecessary.

## Item 51: Define a Root Exception to Insulate Callers from APIs

When you're defining a module's API, the exceptions you throw are just as much a part of your interface as the functions and classes you define (see Item 14: "Prefer Exceptions to Returning `None`").

Python has a built-in hierarchy of exceptions for the language and standard library. There's a draw to using the built-in exception types for reporting errors instead of defining your own new types. For example, you could raise a `ValueError` exception whenever an invalid parameter is passed to your function.

```
def determine_weight(volume, density):
    if density <= 0:
        raise ValueError('Density must be positive')
    # ...
```

In some cases, using `ValueError` makes sense, but for APIs it's much more powerful to define your own hierarchy of exceptions. You can do this by providing a root `Exception` in your module. Then, have all other exceptions raised by that module inherit from the root exception.

```
# my_module.py
class Error(Exception):
    """Base-class for all exceptions raised by this module."""

class InvalidDensityError(Error):
    """There was a problem with a provided density value."""
```

Having a root exception in a module makes it easy for consumers of your API to catch all of the exceptions that you raise on purpose. For example, here a consumer of your API makes a function call with a `try`/`except` statement that catches your root exception:

```
try:
    weight = my_module.determine_weight(1, -1)
except my_module.Error as e:
    logging.error('Unexpected error: %s', e)
```

This `try`/`except` prevents your API's exceptions from propagating too far upward and breaking the calling program. It insulates the calling code from your API. This insulation has three helpful effects.

First, root exceptions let callers understand when there's a problem with their usage of your API. If callers are using your API properly, they should catch the various exceptions that you deliberately raise. If they don't handle such an exception, it will propagate all the way up to the insulating `except` block that catches your module's root exception. That block can bring the exception to the attention of the API consumer, giving them a chance to add proper handling of the exception type.

```
try:
    weight = my_module.determine_weight(1, -1)
except my_module.InvalidDensityError:
    weight = 0
except my_module.Error as e:
    logging.error('Bug in the calling code: %s', e)
```

The second advantage of using root exceptions is that they can help find bugs in your API module's code. If your code only deliberately raises exceptions that you define within your module's hierarchy, then all other types of exceptions raised by your module must be the ones that you didn't intend to raise. These are bugs in your API's code.

Using the `try`/`except` statement above will not insulate API consumers from bugs in your API module's code. To do that, the caller needs to add another `except` block that catches Python's base `Exception` class. This allows the API consumer to detect when there's a bug in the API module's implementation that needs to be fixed.

```
try:
    weight = my_module.determine_weight(1, -1)
except my_module.InvalidDensityError:
    weight = 0
except my_module.Error as e:
    logging.error('Bug in the calling code: %s', e)
except Exception as e:
    logging.error('Bug in the API code: %s', e)
    raise
```

The third impact of using root exceptions is future-proofing your API. Over time, you may want to expand your API to provide more specific exceptions in certain situations. For example, you could add an `Exception` subclass that indicates the error condition of supplying negative densities.

```
# my_module.py
class NegativeDensityError(InvalidDensityError):
    """A provided density value was negative."""

def determine_weight(volume, density):
    if density < 0:
        raise NegativeDensityError
```

The calling code will continue to work exactly as before because it already catches `InvalidDensityError` exceptions (the parent class of `NegativeDensityError`). In the future, the caller could decide to special-case the new type of exception and change its behavior accordingly.

```
try:
    weight = my_module.determine_weight(1, -1)
except my_module.NegativeDensityError as e:
    raise ValueError('Must supply non-negative density') from e
except my_module.InvalidDensityError:
    weight = 0
except my_module.Error as e:
    logging.error('Bug in the calling code: %s', e)
except Exception as e:
    logging.error('Bug in the API code: %s', e)
    raise
```

You can take API future-proofing further by providing a broader set of exceptions directly below the root exception. For example, imagine you had one set of errors related to calculating weights, another related to calculating volume, and a third related to calculating density.

```
# my_module.py
class WeightError(Error):
    """Base-class for weight calculation errors."""

class VolumeError(Error):
    """Base-class for volume calculation errors."""

class DensityError(Error):
    """Base-class for density calculation errors."""
```

Specific exceptions would inherit from these general exceptions. Each intermediate exception acts as its own kind of root exception. This makes it easier to insulate layers of calling code from API code based on broad functionality. This is much better than having all callers catch a long list of very specific `Exception` subclasses.

### Things to Remember

- ✦ Defining root exceptions for your modules allows API consumers to insulate themselves from your API.
- ✦ Catching root exceptions can help you find bugs in code that consumes an API.
- ✦ Catching the Python `Exception` base class can help you find bugs in API implementations.
- ✦ Intermediate root exceptions let you add more specific types of exceptions in the future without breaking your API consumers.

## Item 52: Know How to Break Circular Dependencies

Inevitably, while you're collaborating with others, you'll find a mutual interdependency between modules. It can even happen while you work by yourself on the various parts of a single program.

For example, say you want your GUI application to show a dialog box for choosing where to save a document. The data displayed by the dialog could be specified through arguments to your event handlers. But the dialog also needs to read global state, like user preferences, to know how to render properly.

Here, I define a dialog that retrieves the default document save location from global preferences:

```
# dialog.py
import app
```

```
class Dialog(object):
    def __init__(self, save_dir):
        self.save_dir = save_dir
    # ...

save_dialog = Dialog(app.prefs.get('save_dir'))

def show():
    # ...
```

The problem is that the app module that contains the prefs object also imports the dialog class in order to show the dialog on program start.

```
# app.py
import dialog

class Prefs(object):
    # ...
    def get(self, name):
        # ...

prefs = Prefs()
dialog.show()
```

It's a circular dependency. If you try to use the app module from your main program, you'll get an exception when you import it.

```
Traceback (most recent call last):
  File "main.py", line 4, in <module>
    import app
  File "app.py", line 4, in <module>
    import dialog
  File "dialog.py", line 16, in <module>
    save_dialog = Dialog(app.prefs.get('save_dir'))
AttributeError: 'module' object has no attribute 'prefs'
```

To understand what's happening here, you need to know the details of Python's import machinery. When a module is imported, here's what Python actually does in depth-first order:

1. Searches for your module in locations from sys.path
2. Loads the code from the module and ensures that it compiles
3. Creates a corresponding empty module object
4. Inserts the module into sys.modules
5. Runs the code in the module object to define its contents

The problem with a circular dependency is that the attributes of a module aren't defined until the code for those attributes has executed (after step #5). But the module can be loaded with the `import` statement immediately after it's inserted into `sys.modules` (after step #4).

In the example above, the `app` module imports `dialog` before defining anything. Then, the `dialog` module imports `app`. Since `app` still hasn't finished running—it's currently importing `dialog`—the `app` module is just an empty shell (from step #4). The `AttributeError` is raised (during step #5 for `dialog`) because the code that defines `prefs` hasn't run yet (step #5 for `app` isn't complete).

The best solution to this problem is to refactor your code so that the `prefs` data structure is at the bottom of the dependency tree. Then, both `app` and `dialog` can import the same utility module and avoid any circular dependencies. But such a clear division isn't always possible or could require too much refactoring to be worth the effort.

There are three other ways to break circular dependencies.

### Reordering Imports

The first approach is to change the order of imports. For example, if you import the `dialog` module toward the bottom of the `app` module, after its contents have run, the `AttributeError` goes away.

```
# app.py
class Prefs(object):
    # ...

prefs = Prefs()

import dialog  # Moved
dialog.show()
```

This works because, when the `dialog` module is loaded late, its recursive import of `app` will find that `app.prefs` has already been defined (step #5 is mostly done for `app`).

Although this avoids the `AttributeError`, it goes against the PEP 8 style guide (see Item 2: "Follow the PEP 8 Style Guide"). The style guide suggests that you always put imports at the top of your Python files. This makes your module's dependencies clear to new readers of the code. It also ensures that any module you depend on is in scope and available to all the code in your module.

Having imports later in a file can be brittle and can cause small changes in the ordering of your code to break the module entirely.

Thus, you should avoid import reordering to solve your circular dependency issues.

### Import, Configure, Run

A second solution to the circular imports problem is to have your modules minimize side effects at import time. You have your modules only define functions, classes, and constants. You avoid actually running any functions at import time. Then, you have each module provide a `configure` function that you call once all other modules have finished importing. The purpose of `configure` is to prepare each module's state by accessing the attributes of other modules. You run `configure` after all modules have been imported (step #5 is complete), so all attributes must be defined.

Here, I redefine the `dialog` module to only access the `prefs` object when `configure` is called:

```
# dialog.py
import app

class Dialog(object):
    # ...

save_dialog = Dialog()

def show():
    # ...

def configure():
    save_dialog.save_dir = app.prefs.get('save_dir')
```

I also redefine the `app` module to not run any activities on import.

```
# app.py
import dialog

class Prefs(object):
    # ...

prefs = Prefs()

def configure():
    # ...
```

Finally, the `main` module has three distinct phases of execution: import everything, `configure` everything, and run the first activity.

```
# main.py
import app
import dialog

app.configure()
dialog.configure()

dialog.show()
```

This works well in many situations and enables patterns like *dependency injection*. But sometimes it can be difficult to structure your code so that an explicit `configure` step is possible. Having two distinct phases within a module can also make your code harder to read because it separates the definition of objects from their configuration.

### Dynamic Import

The third—and often simplest—solution to the circular imports problem is to use an `import` statement within a function or method. This is called a *dynamic import* because the module import happens while the program is running, not while the program is first starting up and initializing its modules.

Here, I redefine the `dialog` module to use a dynamic import. The `dialog.show` function imports the `app` module at runtime instead of the `dialog` module importing `app` at initialization time.

```
# dialog.py
class Dialog(object):
    # ...

save_dialog = Dialog()

def show():
    import app  # Dynamic import
    save_dialog.save_dir = app.prefs.get('save_dir')
    # ...
```

The `app` module can now be the same as it was in the original example. It imports `dialog` at the top and calls `dialog.show` at the bottom.

```
# app.py
import dialog

class Prefs(object):
    # ...
```

```
prefs = Prefs()
dialog.show()
```

This approach has a similar effect to the import, configure, and run steps from before. The difference is that this requires no structural changes to the way the modules are defined and imported. You're simply delaying the circular import until the moment you must access the other module. At that point, you can be pretty sure that all other modules have already been initialized (step #5 is complete for everything).

In general, it's good to avoid dynamic imports like this. The cost of the `import` statement is not negligible and can be especially bad in tight loops. By delaying execution, dynamic imports also set you up for surprising failures at runtime, such as `SyntaxError` exceptions long after your program has started running (see Item 56: "Test Everything with `unittest`" for how to avoid that). However, these downsides are often better than the alternative of restructuring your entire program.

### Things to Remember

✦ Circular dependencies happen when two modules must call into each other at import time. They can cause your program to crash at startup.

✦ The best way to break a circular dependency is refactoring mutual dependencies into a separate module at the bottom of the dependency tree.

✦ Dynamic imports are the simplest solution for breaking a circular dependency between modules while minimizing refactoring and complexity.

## Item 53: Use Virtual Environments for Isolated and Reproducible Dependencies

Building larger and more complex programs often leads you to rely on various packages from the Python community (see Item 48: "Know Where to Find Community-Built Modules"). You'll find yourself running `pip` to install packages like `pytz`, `numpy`, and many others.

The problem is that, by default, `pip` installs new packages in a global location. That causes all Python programs on your system to be affected by these installed modules. In theory, this shouldn't be an issue. If you install a package and never `import` it, how could it affect your programs?

The trouble comes from transitive dependencies: the packages that the packages you install depend on. For example, you can see what the Sphinx package depends on after installing it by asking pip.

```
$ pip3 show Sphinx
---
Name: Sphinx
Version: 1.2.2
Location: /usr/local/lib/python3.4/site-packages
Requires: docutils, Jinja2, Pygments
```

If you install another package like flask, you can see that it, too, depends on the Jinja2 package.

```
$ pip3 show flask
---
Name: Flask
Version: 0.10.1
Location: /usr/local/lib/python3.4/site-packages
Requires: Werkzeug, Jinja2, itsdangerous
```

The conflict arises as Sphinx and flask diverge over time. Perhaps right now they both require the same version of Jinja2 and everything is fine. But six months or a year from now, Jinja2 may release a new version that makes breaking changes to users of the library. If you update your global version of Jinja2 with pip install --upgrade, you may find that Sphinx breaks while flask keeps working.

The cause of this breakage is that Python can only have a single global version of a module installed at a time. If one of your installed packages must use the new version and another package must use the old version, your system isn't going to work properly.

Such breakage can even happen when package maintainers try their best to preserve API compatibility between releases (see Item 50: "Use Packages to Organize Modules and Provide Stable APIs"). New versions of a library can subtly change behaviors that API-consuming code relies on. Users on a system may upgrade one package to a new version but not others, which could dependencies. There's a constant risk of the ground moving beneath your feet.

These difficulties are magnified when you collaborate with other developers who do their work on separate computers. It's reasonable to assume that the versions of Python and global packages they have installed on their machines will be slightly different than your own. This can cause frustrating situations where a codebase works perfectly on one programmer's machine and is completely broken on another's.

The solution to all of these problems is a tool called pyvenv, which provides *virtual environments*. Since Python 3.4, the pyvenv command-line tool is available by default along with the Python installation (it's also accessible with python -m venv). Prior versions of Python require installing a separate package (with pip install virtualenv) and using a command-line tool called virtualenv.

pyvenv allows you to create isolated versions of the Python environment. Using pyvenv, you can have many different versions of the same package installed on the same system at the same time without conflicts. This lets you work on many different projects and use many different tools on the same computer.

pyvenv does this by installing explicit versions of packages and their dependencies into completely separate directory structures. This makes it possible to reproduce a Python environment that you know will work with your code. It's a reliable way to avoid surprising breakages.

### The pyvenv Command

Here's a quick tutorial on how to use pyvenv effectively. Before using the tool, it's important to note the meaning of the python3 command-line on your system. On my computer, python3 is located in the /usr/local/bin directory and evaluates to version 3.4.2 (see Item 1: "Know Which Version of Python You're Using").

```
$ which python3
/usr/local/bin/python3
$ python3 --version
Python 3.4.2
```

To demonstrate the setup of my environment, I can test that running a command to import the pytz module doesn't cause an error. This works because I already have the pytz package installed as a global module.

```
$ python3 -c 'import pytz'
$
```

Now, I use pyvenv to create a new virtual environment called myproject. Each virtual environment must live in its own unique directory. The result of the command is a tree of directories and files.

```
$ pyvenv /tmp/myproject
$ cd /tmp/myproject
$ ls
bin     include     lib     pyvenv.cfg
```

To start using the virtual environment, I use the `source` command from my shell on the `bin/activate` script. `activate` modifies all of my environment variables to match the virtual environment. It also updates my command-line prompt to include the virtual environment name ('myproject') to make it extremely clear what I'm working on.

```
$ source bin/activate
(myproject)$
```

After activation, you can see that the path to the `python3` command-line tool has moved to within the virtual environment directory.

```
(myproject)$ which python3
/tmp/myproject/bin/python3
(myproject)$ ls -l /tmp/myproject/bin/python3
... -> /tmp/myproject/bin/python3.4
(myproject)$ ls -l /tmp/myproject/bin/python3.4
... -> /usr/local/bin/python3.4
```

This ensures that changes to the outside system will not affect the virtual environment. Even if the outer system upgrades its default `python3` to version 3.5, my virtual environment will still explicitly point to version 3.4.

The virtual environment I created with `pyvenv` starts with no packages installed except for `pip` and `setuptools`. Trying to use the `pytz` package that was installed as a global module in the outside system will fail because it's unknown to the virtual environment.

```
(myproject)$ python3 -c 'import pytz'
Traceback (most recent call last):
  File "<string>", line 1, in <module>
ImportError: No module named 'pytz'
```

I can use `pip` to install the `pytz` module into my virtual environment.

```
(myproject)$ pip3 install pytz
```

Once it's installed, I can verify that it's working with the same test import command.

```
(myproject)$ python3 -c 'import pytz'
(myproject)$
```

When you're done with a virtual environment and want to go back to your default system, you use the `deactivate` command. This restores your environment to the system defaults, including the location of the `python3` command-line tool.

```
(myproject)$ deactivate
$ which python3
/usr/local/bin/python3
```

If you ever want to work in the `myproject` environment again, you can just run `source bin/activate` in the directory like before.

### Reproducing Dependencies

Once you have a virtual environment, you can continue installing packages with `pip` as you need them. Eventually, you may want to copy your environment somewhere else. For example, say you want to reproduce your development environment on a production server. Or maybe you want to clone someone else's environment on your own machine so you can run their code.

`pyvenv` makes these situations easy. You can use the `pip freeze` command to save all of your explicit package dependencies into a file. By convention, this file is named `requirements.txt`.

```
(myproject)$ pip3 freeze > requirements.txt
(myproject)$ cat requirements.txt
numpy==1.8.2
pytz==2014.4
requests==2.3.0
```

Now, imagine that you'd like to have another virtual environment that matches the `myproject` environment. You can create a new directory like before using `pyvenv` and `activate` it.

```
$ pyvenv /tmp/otherproject
$ cd /tmp/otherproject
$ source bin/activate
(otherproject)$
```

The new environment will have no extra packages installed.

```
(otherproject)$ pip3 list
pip (1.5.6)
setuptools (2.1)
```

You can install all of the packages from the first environment by running `pip install` on the `requirements.txt` that you generated with the `pip freeze` command.

```
(otherproject)$ pip3 install -r /tmp/myproject/requirements.txt
```

This command will crank along for a little while as it retrieves and installs all of the packages required to reproduce the first environment. Once it's done, listing the set of installed packages in the second virtual environment will produce the same list of dependencies found in the first virtual environment.

```
(otherproject)$ pip list
numpy (1.8.2)
pip (1.5.6)
pytz (2014.4)
requests (2.3.0)
setuptools (2.1)
```

Using a `requirements.txt` file is ideal for collaborating with others through a revision control system. You can commit changes to your code at the same time you update your list of package dependencies, ensuring that they move in lockstep.

The gotcha with virtual environments is that moving them breaks everything because all of the paths, like `python3`, are hard-coded to the environment's install directory. But that doesn't matter. The whole purpose of virtual environments is to make it easy to reproduce the same setup. Instead of moving a virtual environment directory, just `freeze` the old one, create a new one somewhere else, and reinstall everything from the `requirements.txt` file.

### Things to Remember

- ✦ Virtual environments allow you to use `pip` to install many different versions of the same package on the same machine without conflicts.
- ✦ Virtual environments are created with `pyvenv`, enabled with `source bin/activate`, and disabled with `deactivate`.
- ✦ You can dump all of the requirements of an environment with `pip freeze`. You can reproduce the environment by supplying the `requirements.txt` file to `pip install -r`.
- ✦ In versions of Python before 3.4, the `pyvenv` tool must be downloaded and installed separately. The command-line tool is called `virtualenv` instead of `pyvenv`.

# 8 Production

Putting a Python program to use requires moving it from a development environment to a production environment. Supporting disparate configurations like this can be a challenge. Making programs that are dependable in multiple situations is just as important as making programs with correct functionality.

The goal is to *productionize* your Python programs and make them bulletproof while they're in use. Python has built-in modules that aid in hardening your programs. It provides facilities for debugging, optimizing, and testing to maximize the quality and performance of your programs at runtime.

## Item 54: Consider Module-Scoped Code to Configure Deployment Environments

A deployment environment is a configuration in which your program runs. Every program has at least one deployment environment, the *production environment*. The goal of writing a program in the first place is to put it to work in the production environment and achieve some kind of outcome.

Writing or modifying a program requires being able to run it on the computer you use for developing. The configuration of your *development environment* may be much different from your production environment. For example, you may be writing a program for supercomputers using a Linux workstation.

Tools like `pyvenv` (see Item 53: "Use Virtual Environments for Isolated and Reproducible Dependencies") make it easy to ensure that all environments have the same Python packages installed. The trouble is that production environments often require many external assumptions that are hard to reproduce in development environments.

For example, say you want to run your program in a web server container and give it access to a database. This means that every time you want to modify your program's code, you need to run a server container, the database must be set up properly, and your program needs the password for access. That's a very high cost if all you're trying to do is verify that a one-line change to your program works correctly.

The best way to work around these issues is to override parts of your program at startup time to provide different functionality depending on the deployment environment. For example, you could have two different `__main__` files, one for production and one for development.

```
# dev_main.py
TESTING = True
import db_connection
db = db_connection.Database()
```

```
# prod_main.py
TESTING = False
import db_connection
db = db_connection.Database()
```

The only difference between the two files is the value of the `TESTING` constant. Other modules in your program can then import the `__main__` module and use the value of `TESTING` to decide how they define their own attributes.

```
# db_connection.py
import __main__

class TestingDatabase(object):
    # ...

class RealDatabase(object):
    # ...

if __main__.TESTING:
    Database = TestingDatabase
else:
    Database = RealDatabase
```

The key behavior to notice here is that code running in module scope—not inside any function or method—is just normal Python code. You can use an `if` statement at the module level to decide how the module will define names. This makes it easy to tailor modules to your various deployment environments. You can avoid having to reproduce costly assumptions like database configurations when they aren't needed. You can inject fake or mock implementations that ease interactive development and testing (see Item 56: "Test Everything with `unittest`").

> **Note**
>
> Once your deployment environments get complicated, you should consider moving them out of Python constants (like TESTING) and into dedicated configuration files. Tools like the `configparser` built-in module let you maintain production configurations separate from code, a distinction that's crucial for collaborating with an operations team.

This approach can be used for more than working around external assumptions. For example, if you know that your program must work differently based on its host platform, you can inspect the sys module before defining top-level constructs in a module.

```
# db_connection.py
import sys

class Win32Database(object):
    # ...

class PosixDatabase(object):
    # ...

if sys.platform.startswith('win32'):
    Database = Win32Database
else:
    Database = PosixDatabase
```

Similarly, you can use environment variables from `os.environ` to guide your module definitions.

### Things to Remember

- ✦ Programs often need to run in multiple deployment environments that each have unique assumptions and configurations.
- ✦ You can tailor a module's contents to different deployment environments by using normal Python statements in module scope.
- ✦ Module contents can be the product of any external condition, including host introspection through the sys and os modules.

## Item 55: Use repr Strings for Debugging Output

When debugging a Python program, the print function (or output via the logging built-in module) will get you surprisingly far. Python internals are often easy to access via plain attributes (see Item 27: "Prefer Public Attributes Over Private Ones"). All you need to do is print how the state of your program changes while it runs and see where it goes wrong.

The print function outputs a human-readable string version of whatever you supply it. For example, printing a basic string will print the contents of the string without the surrounding quote characters.

```
print('foo bar')
>>>
foo bar
```

This is equivalent to using the '%s' format string and the % operator.

```
print('%s' % 'foo bar')
>>>
foo bar
```

The problem is that the human-readable string for a value doesn't make it clear what the actual type of the value is. For example, notice how in the default output of print you can't distinguish between the types of the number 5 and the string '5'.

```
print(5)
print('5')

>>>
5
5
```

If you're debugging a program with print, these type differences matter. What you almost always want while debugging is to see the repr version of an object. The repr built-in function returns the *printable representation* of an object, which should be its most clearly understandable string representation. For built-in types, the string returned by repr is a valid Python expression.

```
a = '\x07'
print(repr(a))

>>>
'\x07'
```

Passing the value from repr to the eval built-in function should result in the same Python object you started with (of course, in practice, you should only use eval with extreme caution).

```
b = eval(repr(a))
assert a == b
```

When you're debugging with print, you should repr the value before printing to ensure that any difference in types is clear.

```
print(repr(5))
print(repr('5'))

>>>
5
'5'
```

This is equivalent to using the '%r' format string and the % operator.

```
print('%r' % 5)
print('%r' % '5')

>>>
5
'5'
```

For dynamic Python objects, the default human-readable string value is the same as the repr value. This means that passing a dynamic object to print will do the right thing, and you don't need to explicitly call repr on it. Unfortunately, the default value of repr for object instances isn't especially helpful. For example, here I define a simple class and then print its value:

```
class OpaqueClass(object):
    def __init__(self, x, y):
        self.x = x
        self.y = y

obj = OpaqueClass(1, 2)
print(obj)

>>>
<__main__.OpaqueClass object at 0x107880ba8>
```

This output can't be passed to the eval function, and it says nothing about the instance fields of the object.

There are two solutions to this problem. If you have control of the class, you can define your own __repr__ special method that returns a string containing the Python expression that recreates the object. Here, I define that function for the class above:

```
class BetterClass(object):
    def __init__(self, x, y):
        # ...

    def __repr__(self):
        return 'BetterClass(%d, %d)' % (self.x, self.y)
```

Now, the `repr` value is much more useful.

```
obj = BetterClass(1, 2)
print(obj)

>>>
BetterClass(1, 2)
```

When you don't have control over the class definition, you can reach into the object's instance dictionary, which is stored in the `__dict__` attribute. Here, I print out the contents of an `OpaqueClass` instance:

```
obj = OpaqueClass(4, 5)
print(obj.__dict__)

>>>
{'y': 5, 'x': 4}
```

## Things to Remember

- ✦ Calling `print` on built-in Python types will produce the human-readable string version of a value, which hides type information.
- ✦ Calling `repr` on built-in Python types will produce the printable string version of a value. These `repr` strings could be passed to the `eval` built-in function to get back the original value.
- ✦ `%s` in format strings will produce human-readable strings like `str`. `%r` will produce printable strings like `repr`.
- ✦ You can define the `__repr__` method to customize the printable representation of a class and provide more detailed debugging information.
- ✦ You can reach into any object's `__dict__` attribute to view its internals.

## Item 56: Test Everything with `unittest`

Python doesn't have static type checking. There's nothing in the compiler that will ensure that your program will work when you run it.

With Python you don't know whether the functions your program calls will be defined at runtime, even when their existence is evident in the source code. This dynamic behavior is a blessing and a curse.

The large numbers of Python programmers out there say it's worth it because of the productivity gained from the resulting brevity and simplicity. But most people have heard at least one horror story about Python in which a program encountered a boneheaded error at runtime.

One of the worst examples I've heard is when a `SyntaxError` was raised in production as a side effect of a dynamic import (see Item 52: "Know How to Break Circular Dependencies"). The programmer I know who was hit by this surprising occurrence has since ruled out using Python ever again.

But I have to wonder, why wasn't the code tested before the program was deployed to production? Type safety isn't everything. You should always test your code, regardless of what language it's written in. However, I'll admit that the big difference between Python and many other languages is that the only way to have *any* confidence in a Python program is by writing tests. There is no veil of static type checking to make you feel safe.

Luckily, the same dynamic features that prevent static type checking in Python also make it extremely easy to write tests for your code. You can use Python's dynamic nature and easily overridable behaviors to implement tests and ensure that your programs work as expected.

You should think of tests as an insurance policy on your code. Good tests give you confidence that your code is correct. If you refactor or expand your code, tests make it easy to identify how behaviors have changed. It sounds counter-intuitive, but having good tests actually makes it easier to modify Python code, not harder.

The simplest way to write tests is to use the `unittest` built-in module. For example, say you have the following utility function defined in `utils.py`:

```
# utils.py
def to_str(data):
    if isinstance(data, str):
        return data
    elif isinstance(data, bytes):
        return data.decode('utf-8')
    else:
        raise TypeError('Must supply str or bytes, '
                        'found: %r' % data)
```

To define tests, I create a second file named `test_utils.py` or `utils_test.py` that contains tests for each behavior I expect.

```
# utils_test.py
from unittest import TestCase, main
from utils import to_str

class UtilsTestCase(TestCase):
    def test_to_str_bytes(self):
        self.assertEqual('hello', to_str(b'hello'))

    def test_to_str_str(self):
        self.assertEqual('hello', to_str('hello'))

    def test_to_str_bad(self):
        self.assertRaises(TypeError, to_str, object())

if __name__ == '__main__':
    main()
```

Tests are organized into `TestCase` classes. Each test is a method beginning with the word `test`. If a test method runs without raising any kind of `Exception` (including `AssertionError` from `assert` statements), then the test is considered to have passed successfully.

The `TestCase` class provides helper methods for making assertions in your tests, such as `assertEqual` for verifying equality, `assertTrue` for verifying Boolean expressions, and `assertRaises` for verifying that exceptions are raised when appropriate (see `help(TestCase)` for more). You can define your own helper methods in `TestCase` subclasses to make your tests more readable; just ensure that your method names don't begin with the word `test`.

> **Note**
>
> Another common practice when writing tests is to use mock functions and classes to stub out certain behaviors. For this purpose, Python 3 provides the `unittest.mock` built-in module, which is also available for Python 2 as an open source package.

Sometimes, your `TestCase` classes need to set up the test environment before running test methods. To do this, you can override the `setUp` and `tearDown` methods. These methods are called before and after each test method, respectively, and they let you ensure that each test runs in isolation (an important best practice of proper testing). For example, here I define a TestCase that creates a temporary directory before each test and deletes its contents after each test finishes:

```
class MyTest(TestCase):
    def setUp(self):
        self.test_dir = TemporaryDirectory()
    def tearDown(self):
        self.test_dir.cleanup()
    # Test methods follow
    # ...
```

I usually define one TestCase for each set of related tests. Sometimes I have one TestCase for each function that has many edge cases. Other times, a TestCase spans all functions in a single module. I'll also create one TestCase for testing a single class and all of its methods.

When programs get complicated, you'll want additional tests for verifying the interactions between your modules, instead of only testing code in isolation. This is the difference between *unit tests* and *integration tests*. In Python, it's important to write both types of tests for exactly the same reason: You have no guarantee that your modules will actually work together unless you prove it.

> **Note**
>
> Depending on your project, it can also be useful to define data-driven tests or organize tests into different suites of related functionality. For these purposes, code coverage reports, and other advanced use cases, the nose (http://nose.readthedocs.org/) and pytest (http://pytest.org/) open source packages can be especially helpful.

**Things to Remember**

- ✦ The only way to have confidence in a Python program is to write tests.
- ✦ The unittest built-in module provides most of the facilities you'll need to write good tests.
- ✦ You can define tests by subclassing TestCase and defining one method per behavior you'd like to test. Test methods on TestCase classes must start with the word test.
- ✦ It's important to write both unit tests (for isolated functionality) and integration tests (for modules that interact).

## Item 57: Consider Interactive Debugging with pdb

Everyone encounters bugs in their code while developing programs. Using the print function can help you track down the source of many issues (see Item 55: "Use repr Strings for Debugging Output"). Writing tests for specific cases that cause trouble is another great way to isolate problems (see Item 56: "Test Everything with unittest").

But these tools aren't enough to find every root cause. When you need something more powerful, it's time to try Python's built-in *interactive debugger.* The debugger lets you inspect program state, print local variables, and step through a Python program one statement at a time.

In most other programming languages, you use a debugger by specifying what line of a source file you'd like to stop on, then execute the program. In contrast, with Python the easiest way to use the debugger is by modifying your program to directly initiate the debugger just before you think you'll have an issue worth investigating. There is no difference between running a Python program under a debugger and running it normally.

To initiate the debugger, all you have to do is import the pdb built-in module and run its set_trace function. You'll often see this done in a single line so programmers can comment it out with a single # character.

```
def complex_func(a, b, c):
    # ...
    import pdb; pdb.set_trace()
```

As soon as this statement runs, the program will pause its execution. The terminal that started your program will turn into an interactive Python shell.

```
-> import pdb; pdb.set_trace()
(Pdb)
```

At the (Pdb) prompt, you can type in the name of local variables to see their values printed out. You can see a list of all local variables by calling the locals built-in function. You can import modules, inspect global state, construct new objects, run the help built-in function, and even modify parts of the program—whatever you need to do to aid in your debugging. In addition, the debugger has three commands that make inspecting the running program easier.

- bt: Print the traceback of the current execution call stack. This lets you figure out where you are in your program and how you arrived at the pdb.set_trace trigger point.

- `up`: Move your scope up the function call stack to the caller of the current function. This allows you to inspect the local variables in higher levels of the call stack.
- `down`: Move your scope back down the function call stack one level.

Once you're done inspecting the current state, you can use debugger commands to resume the program's execution under precise control.

- `step`: Run the program until the next line of execution in the program, then return control back to the debugger. If the next line of execution includes calling a function, the debugger will stop in the function that was called.
- `next`: Run the program until the next line of execution in the current function, then return control back to the debugger. If the next line of execution includes calling a function, the debugger will not stop until the called function has returned.
- `return`: Run the program until the current function returns, then return control back to the debugger.
- `continue`: Continue running the program until the next breakpoint (or `set_trace` is called again).

### Things to Remember

✦ You can initiate the Python interactive debugger at a point of interest directly in your program with the `import pdb; pdb.set_trace()` statements.

✦ The Python debugger prompt is a full Python shell that lets you inspect and modify the state of a running program.

✦ `pdb` shell commands let you precisely control program execution, allowing you to alternate between inspecting program state and progressing program execution.

## Item 58: Profile Before Optimizing

The dynamic nature of Python causes surprising behaviors in its runtime performance. Operations you might assume are slow are actually very fast (string manipulation, generators). Language features you might assume are fast are actually very slow (attribute access, function calls). The true source of slowdowns in a Python program can be obscure.

The best approach is to ignore your intuition and directly measure the performance of a program before you try to optimize it. Python provides a built-in *profiler* for determining which parts of a program are responsible for its execution time. This lets you focus your optimization efforts on the biggest sources of trouble and ignore parts of the program that don't impact speed.

For example, say you want to determine why an algorithm in your program is slow. Here, I define a function that sorts a list of data using an insertion sort:

```
def insertion_sort(data):
    result = []
    for value in data:
        insert_value(result, value)
    return result
```

The core mechanism of the insertion sort is the function that finds the insertion point for each piece of data. Here, I define an extremely inefficient version of the insert_value function that does a linear scan over the input array:

```
def insert_value(array, value):
    for i, existing in enumerate(array):
        if existing > value:
            array.insert(i, value)
            return
    array.append(value)
```

To profile insertion_sort and insert_value, I create a data set of random numbers and define a test function to pass to the profiler.

```
from random import randint

max_size = 10**4
data = [randint(0, max_size) for _ in range(max_size)]
test = lambda: insertion_sort(data)
```

Python provides two built-in profilers, one that is pure Python (profile) and another that is a C-extension module (cProfile). The cProfile built-in module is better because of its minimal impact on the performance of your program while it's being profiled. The pure-Python alternative imposes a high overhead that will skew the results.

### Note

When profiling a Python program, be sure that what you're measuring is the code itself and not any external systems. Beware of functions that access the network or resources on disk. These may appear to have a large impact on your program's execution time because of the slowness of the underlying systems.

If your program uses a cache to mask the latency of slow resources like these, you should also ensure that it's properly warmed up before you start profiling.

Here, I instantiate a `Profile` object from the `cProfile` module and run the test function through it using the `runcall` method:

```
profiler = Profile()
profiler.runcall(test)
```

Once the test function has finished running, I can extract statistics about its performance using the `pstats` built-in module and its `Stats` class. Various methods on a `Stats` object adjust how to select and sort the profiling information to show only the things you care about.

```
stats = Stats(profiler)
stats.strip_dirs()
stats.sort_stats('cumulative')
stats.print_stats()
```

The output is a table of information organized by function. The data sample is taken only from the time the profiler was active, during the `runcall` method above.

```
>>>
         20003 function calls in 1.812 seconds

   Ordered by: cumulative time

   ncalls  tottime  percall  cumtime  percall filename:lineno(function)
        1    0.000    0.000    1.812    1.812 main.py:34(<lambda>)
        1    0.003    0.003    1.812    1.812 main.py:10(insertion_sort)
    10000    1.797    0.000    1.810    0.000 main.py:20(insert_value)
     9992    0.013    0.000    0.013    0.000 {method 'insert' of 'list' objects}
        8    0.000    0.000    0.000    0.000 {method 'append' of 'list' objects}
        1    0.000    0.000    0.000    0.000 {method 'disable' of '_lsprof.Profiler' objects}
```

Here's a quick guide to what the profiler statistics columns mean:

- `ncalls`: The number of calls to the function during the profiling period.
- `tottime`: The number of seconds spent executing the function, excluding time spent executing other functions it calls.
- `tottime percall`: The average number of seconds spent in the function each time it was called, excluding time spent executing other functions it calls. This is `tottime` divided by `ncalls`.
- `cumtime`: The cumulative number of seconds spent executing the function, including time spent in all other functions it calls.
- `cumtime percall`: The average number of seconds spent in the function each time it was called, including time spent in all other functions it calls. This is `cumtime` divided by `ncalls`.

Looking at the profiler statistics table above, I can see that the biggest use of CPU in my test is the cumulative time spent in the `insert_value` function. Here, I redefine that function to use the `bisect` built-in module (see Item 46: "Use Built-in Algorithms and Data Structures"):

```
from bisect import bisect_left

def insert_value(array, value):
    i = bisect_left(array, value)
    array.insert(i, value)
```

I can run the profiler again and generate a new table of profiler statistics. The new function is much faster, with a cumulative time spent that is nearly 100× smaller than the previous `insert_value` function.

```
>>>
         30003 function calls in 0.028 seconds

   Ordered by: cumulative time

   ncalls  tottime  percall  cumtime  percall filename:lineno(function)
        1    0.000    0.000    0.028    0.028 main.py:34(<lambda>)
        1    0.002    0.002    0.028    0.028 main.py:10(insertion_sort)
    10000    0.005    0.000    0.026    0.000 main.py:112(insert_value)
    10000    0.014    0.000    0.014    0.000 {method 'insert' of 'list' objects}
    10000    0.007    0.000    0.007    0.000 {built-in method bisect_left}
        1    0.000    0.000    0.000    0.000 {method 'disable' of '_lsprof.Profiler' objects}
```

Sometimes, when you're profiling an entire program, you'll find that a common utility function is responsible for the majority of execution time. The default output from the profiler makes this situation difficult to understand because it doesn't show how the utility function is called by many different parts of your program.

For example, here the `my_utility` function is called repeatedly by two different functions in the program:

```
def my_utility(a, b):
    # ...

def first_func():
    for _ in range(1000):
        my_utility(4, 5)

def second_func():
    for _ in range(10):
        my_utility(1, 3)

def my_program():
    for _ in range(20):
        first_func()
        second_func()
```

Profiling this code and using the default `print_stats` output will generate output statistics that are confusing.

```
>>>
         20242 function calls in 0.208 seconds

   Ordered by: cumulative time

   ncalls  tottime  percall  cumtime  percall filename:lineno(function)
        1    0.000    0.000    0.208    0.208 main.py:176(my_program)
       20    0.005    0.000    0.206    0.010 main.py:168(first_func)
    20200    0.203    0.000    0.203    0.000 main.py:161(my_utility)
       20    0.000    0.000    0.002    0.000 main.py:172(second_func)
        1    0.000    0.000    0.000    0.000 {method 'disable' of '_lsprof.Profiler' objects}
```

The `my_utility` function is clearly the source of most execution time, but it's not immediately obvious why that function is called so much. If you search through the program's code, you'll find multiple call sites for `my_utility` and still be confused.

To deal with this, the Python profiler provides a way of seeing which callers contributed to the profiling information of each function.

```
stats.print_callers()
```

This profiler statistics table shows functions called on the left and who was responsible for making the call on the right. Here, it's clear that `my_utility` is most used by `first_func`:

```
>>>
   Ordered by: cumulative time

Function                                          was called by...
                                                      ncalls  tottime  cumtime
main.py:176(my_program)                           <-
main.py:168(first_func)                           <-      20    0.005    0.206  main.py:176(my_program)
main.py:161(my_utility)                           <-   20000    0.202    0.202  main.py:168(first_func)
                                                         200    0.002    0.002  main.py:172(second_func)
main.py:172(second_func)                          <-      20    0.000    0.002  main.py:176(my_program)
```

### Things to Remember

- ✦ It's important to profile Python programs before optimizing because the source of slowdowns is often obscure.
- ✦ Use the `cProfile` module instead of the `profile` module because it provides more accurate profiling information.
- ✦ The `Profile` object's `runcall` method provides everything you need to profile a tree of function calls in isolation.
- ✦ The `Stats` object lets you select and print the subset of profiling information you need to see to understand your program's performance.

## Item 59: Use tracemalloc to Understand Memory Usage and Leaks

Memory management in the default implementation of Python, CPython, uses reference counting. This ensures that as soon as all references to an object have expired, the referenced object is also cleared. CPython also has a built-in cycle detector to ensure that self-referencing objects are eventually garbage collected.

In theory, this means that most Python programmers don't have to worry about allocating or deallocating memory in their programs. It's taken care of automatically by the language and the CPython runtime. However, in practice, programs eventually do run out of memory due to held references. Figuring out where your Python programs are using or leaking memory proves to be a challenge.

The first way to debug memory usage is to ask the gc built-in module to list every object currently known by the garbage collector. Although it's quite a blunt tool, this approach does let you quickly get a sense of where your program's memory is being used.

Here, I run a program that wastes memory by keeping references. It prints out how many objects were created during execution and a small sample of allocated objects.

```
# using_gc.py
import gc
found_objects = gc.get_objects()
print('%d objects before' % len(found_objects))

import waste_memory
x = waste_memory.run()
found_objects = gc.get_objects()
print('%d objects after' % len(found_objects))
for obj in found_objects[:3]:
    print(repr(obj)[:100])

>>>
4756 objects before
14873 objects after
<waste_memory.MyObject object at 0x1063f6940>
<waste_memory.MyObject object at 0x1063f6978>
<waste_memory.MyObject object at 0x1063f69b0>
```

The problem with gc.get_objects is that it doesn't tell you anything about *how* the objects were allocated. In complicated programs, a specific class of object could be allocated many different ways. The overall number of objects isn't nearly as important as identifying the code responsible for allocating the objects that are leaking memory.

Python 3.4 introduces a new tracemalloc built-in module for solving this problem. tracemalloc makes it possible to connect an object back to where it was allocated. Here, I print out the top three memory usage offenders in a program using tracemalloc:

```
# top_n.py
import tracemalloc
tracemalloc.start(10)  # Save up to 10 stack frames

time1 = tracemalloc.take_snapshot()
import waste_memory
x = waste_memory.run()
time2 = tracemalloc.take_snapshot()

stats = time2.compare_to(time1, 'lineno')
for stat in stats[:3]:
    print(stat)

>>>
waste_memory.py:6: size=2235 KiB (+2235 KiB), count=29981 (+29981), average=76 B
waste_memory.py:7: size=869 KiB (+869 KiB), count=10000 (+10000), average=89 B
waste_memory.py:12: size=547 KiB (+547 KiB), count=10000 (+10000), average=56 B
```

It's immediately clear which objects are dominating my program's memory usage and where in the source code they were allocated.

The tracemalloc module can also print out the full stack trace of each allocation (up to the number of frames passed to the start method). Here, I print out the stack trace of the biggest source of memory usage in the program:

```
# with_trace.py
# ...
stats = time2.compare_to(time1, 'traceback')
top = stats[0]
print('\n'.join(top.traceback.format()))

>>>
File "waste_memory.py", line 6
  self.x = os.urandom(100)
File "waste_memory.py", line 12
  obj = MyObject()
File "waste_memory.py", line 19
  deep_values.append(get_data())
```

```
File "with_trace.py", line 10
  x = waste_memory.run()
```

A stack trace like this is most valuable for figuring out which particular usage of a common function is responsible for memory consumption in a program.

Unfortunately, Python 2 doesn't provide the `tracemalloc` built-in module. There are open source packages for tracking memory usage in Python 2 (such as `heapy`), though they do not fully replicate the functionality of `tracemalloc`.

### Things to Remember

- ✦ It can be difficult to understand how Python programs use and leak memory.
- ✦ The `gc` module can help you understand which objects exist, but it has no information about how they were allocated.
- ✦ The `tracemalloc` built-in module provides powerful tools for understanding the source of memory usage.
- ✦ `tracemalloc` is only available in Python 3.4 and above.

# Index

## Symbols



## A



## B



## C

## Y



## Z